ISSUES IN MULTINATIONAL ACCOUNTING

C. W. Nobes and R. H. Parker

Philip Allan/St Martin's Press

First published 1988 by

PHILIP ALLAN PUBLISHERS LIMITED
MARKET PLACE
DEDDINGTON
OXFORD OX5 4SE

First published in the USA 1988 by

ST MARTIN'S PRESS, INC.
SCHOLARLY & REFERENCE BOOKS DIVISION
175 FIFTH AVENUE
NEW YORK, N.Y. 10010

British Library Cataloguing in Publication Data

Nobes, Christopher
Issues in multinational accounting.
1. Multinational companies. Accounting
I. Title II. Parker, R.H. (Robert Henry)
657'.95

ISBN 0–86003–551–4
ISBN 0–86003–654–5 Pbk

Library of Congress Cataloging-in-Publication Data

Nobes, Christopher.
Issues in multinational accounting / Christopher W. Nobes and
Robert H. Parker.
p. cm.
Bibliography: p.
Includes index.
ISBN 0–312–02363–4 (U.S.) : $40.00 (est.)
1. Comparative accounting. 2. International business enterprises –
–Accounting. I. Parker, R.H. (Robert Henry) II. Title.
HF5625.N64 1988
657—dc 19

Typeset by Dataset Marlborough Design, St Clements, Oxford
Printed and bound by Bookcraft (Bath) Limited

Contents

Contributors

Co-editor, author of Chapters 2 and 3, and co-author of Chapter 5:

Christopher W. Nobes Deloitte Professor of Accounting at the University of Reading. Has also taught in Scotland, the USA, Australia and New Zealand. Member of the Accounting Standards Committee of the UK and Ireland, and of a committee of the *Fédération des Experts Comptables Européens*. Joint editor of *Accounting and Business Research*.

Co-editor, author of Chapter 4, and co-author of Chapter 5:

Robert H. Parker Professor of Accountancy at the University of Exeter. Has also practised and taught in Nigeria, Australia, France and Scotland. Joint editor of *Accounting and Business Research*.

Authors of Other Chapters:

Jeffrey S. Arpan Professor and Director of International Business Programs at the University of South Carolina. Formerly vice-president of the Academy of International Business. (Chapter 8)

John H. Dunning ICI Research Professor in International Business at the University of Reading. Author of 22 books and monographs on foreign direct investment and the multinational enterprise. President of the Academy of International Business, 1987/88. (Chapter 1)

Sidney J. Gray Professor of Accounting and Finance at the University of Glasgow. Joint managing editor of *Journal of International Financial Management and Accounting*. Vice President (Europe) of the International Association of Accounting Education and Research. (Chapter 6)

Stuart J. McLeay TSB Professor of Treasury at the University College of North Wales, Bangor. Formerly worked as a chartered accountant in Germany, France and Italy, and was a financial analyst at the European Investment Bank. (Chapter 7)

Robert D. Pearce Senior Research Fellow, Department of Economics at the University of Reading. (Chapter 1)

Clare B. Roberts Lecturer in Accounting and Finance at the University of Glasgow. (Chapter 6)

Preface

This book is intended to complement *Comparative International Accounting* (2nd edn, 1985). It takes up and develops some of the themes from that book and also introduces new ones.

We identified, in our previous book, four reasons for studying international accounting: the historical development of modern accounting in many different countries; the growth in importance of the multinational enterprise (MNE); the benefits to be gained by comparing financial reporting systems across countries; and the spread of harmonisation. The emphasis in the present book is on the MNE, on comparative financial reporting in countries in which MNEs are based, and on accounting problems of especial importance to MNEs. The spread of harmonisation is also examined, particularly in Chapter 5.

Part I contains an introduction to multinational enterprises, wherein Dunning and Pearce set the scene by looking at the nature and growth of MNEs. One of the points they bring out is the importance of intra-group trade. Such trade leads to particular accounting problems, discussed in Part III.

Part II, entirely by the editors, deals with some problems of comparative financial reporting, particularly in countries where MNEs are based. Despite all attempts at harmonisation, major differences remain. Chapter 2 identifies and discusses seven causes of these differences. Chapter 3 goes on to look at the type and content of the differences. Whereas these chapters tend to stress the similarities between financial reporting in the major Anglo-Saxon countries (UK, USA, Australia, Canada), Chapter 4 draws attention to the differences, emphasising that, whereas economic forces have led to similar financial reporting practices, political factors have resulted in rather different regulatory frameworks.

Part III is concerned with accounting problems that come into being or are particularly severe for MNEs. One such international difference, already introduced in Chapter 3, relates to the practice, concepts and techniques of consolidation accounting. This is discussed by the editors in more detail in Chapter 5, which looks at the way in which consolidated financial statements both within the EEC and outside its boundaries will be affected by the implementation of the seventh Directive. MNEs are usually not only multinational but also multiproduct, thus requiring, it can be argued, a matrix form of corporate financial reporting. This problem results, of course, from the way in which consolidation tries to summarise data. The topic of segmental reporting, including its costs and benefits and the need for regulation, is analysed by Gray and Roberts in Chapter 6. The growth of MNEs has led to an international capital market in which international investors seek to apply the same techniques of investment analysis as they use in domestic ones. The problems and perils of this, particularly resulting from the differences examined earlier, are discussed by McLeay in Chapter 7. Multinational trade also brings with it the critical problem of the pricing on inter-corporate transfers. This is the subject of Chapter 8 by Arpan who looks especially at the empirical studies which have been made of international transfer pricing and at the impact of governments.

We were talked into writing and editing this book by Philip Allan whose publishing house remains in our view an exemplar for others to copy. We are grateful also to our fellow contributors — Jeff Arpan, John Dunning, Sid Gray, Stuart McLeay, Bob Pearce and Clare Roberts — for writing their respective chapters and responding positively to our editorial suggestions. In writing Chapters 4 and 5, the editors faced the usual problem in international accounting of ensuring that the facts were both correct and up-to-date. In this we were helped by Ken Lemke, Graham Peirson, Paul Rutteman and Steve Zeff. They are in no way responsible for any errors that remain or for any expressions of opinion. For the processing of words we are grateful to Elvy Ibbotson and Meg Wells.

May 1988

R.H. Parker
C.W. Nobes

Part I
INTRODUCTION

1
The Nature and Growth of MNEs

JOHN H. DUNNING
ROBERT D. PEARCE

1.1 Definitions and Distinctions

In this introductory section, we provide a broad definition of the Multinational Enterprise (MNE), and of the related concept of foreign direct investment (FDI). We then attempt to identify various types of MNE by their distinctive industrial and operational characteristics.

We may define an MNE as 'an enterprise that owns and controls value-adding activities in more than one country'. As well as acknowledging the geographical dispersion of their activities, this definition also recognises that such firms may produce both goods and services. Indeed an increasing proportion of MNE activity is now being directed to the service industries (UNCTC, 1988). No less relevant is the fact that firms whose predominant activity remains in the primary or secondary sector are showing a growing tendency to globalise many of their support functions. These may include not only the more familiar marketing and distribution operations, but also such potentially high value activities as R & D and innovation (see Pearce, 1987).

Another brief definition describes MNEs as 'firms that engage in foreign direct investment' (Dunning, 1981, p.3). Direct investment is defined in the IMF Balance of Payments Manual (IMF, 1977, p.136) as 'investment that is made to acquire a lasting interest in an enterprise operating in an economy other than that of the investor, the investor's purpose being to have an effective voice in the management of the enterprise'. In this definition FDI is contrasted with portfolio investment, where the motivation of the investor is limited to financial gain. The retention of what appears to be essentially a financial concept at the centre of the MNE perhaps requires comment. It is generally agreed that the competitive advantages possessed by MNEs lie less in their ability to obtain or utilise finance capital, and more in their comparative advantage in acquiring and organising non-financial assets such as technology, know-how, skills (management, marketing), trademarks, etc. Moreover the evidence strongly suggests that established MNEs choose to finance new overseas subsidiaries, or foreign affiliate growth, primarily from funds obtained on the local or international capital markets, or from reinvested earnings. Nevertheless it remains true that, with the various intangible assets adequately valued, the overseas affiliates are direct investments as defined by the IMF. This clarification is also relevant since, as we shall see, estimates of the global activities of MNEs are based mainly on FDI data; information on other indices (e.g. sales, value-added, employment) is rarely available.

Let us now turn to consider the main kinds of activities in which MNEs are involved. Although we describe these categories separately we accept that in practice an MNE might be involved in several of them simultaneously and that, over time, MNEs may switch their main emphasis from one activity to another. Nevertheless, as a means of delineating the scope of MNEs, and relating the factors influencing their modes of operation, we believe the categorisation may prove helpful. The organisation of the information derived within such a listing into a comprehensive analytical framework is described below (see Section 1.4).

(i) Resource-Based Activities (the resource-seeking MNEs)

Though notably in decline in recent decades, the activity of MNEs to gain access to the natural resources of certain countries was the major *raison d'être* of FDI for much of the 19th century. In both mines and plantations, MNEs were prevalent in the production of, for example, oil, copper, tin, zinc, bauxite, bananas, pineapples, cocoa and tea. In many cases the MNEs were vertically integrated and were motivated to operate at the primary stage by the desire to achieve security of raw materials supply. In addition, the MNEs' superior access to capital, technology and global markets put them in a stronger position to develop these resources more efficiently than potential local enterprises.

(ii) Import-Substituting Manufacturing (the market-seeking MNEs)

In this case the MNE subsidiary aims to produce goods predominantly for supply to the market of the country in which it is located. Assuming that the MNE possesses advantages that make it a competitive supplier to the particular market (technology, management and organisational skills, familiar trademarks, etc.) a whole range of locational influences may contribute to its decision to produce within the country, rather than export to it from some other source. These may be natural restraints to trade (i.e. transport costs) or encouragements to local production, such as low-cost labour or other favourable input supplies. In addition this type of direct investment may be deliberately induced by governments as part of a programme of import-substituting industrialisation, e.g. by such means as tariffs or other import restraints, and investment incentives. The decision to undertake import-substituting manufacturing also suggests that the option of transferring the crucial productive asset to a local enterprise for a suitable fee has been rejected. The reason for avoiding this alternative (and thus retaining the use of the advantage within the MNE) varies between industries. Where a globally familiar and respected trademark is important (e.g. in the case of cigarettes or cornflakes) the fear of having this asset undermined by sub-standard licensed production encourages the retention of control over production. However, it would be wrong to equate import-substituting manufacturing with low-level standardised technology. It may also occur in such innovation-driven industries as pharmaceuticals, where the MNE may wish to retain maximum control over the economic rents accruing from such creativity. In other relatively high-technology industries (e.g. consumer electronics), the failure to transfer knowledge assets between firms (and thus the sustained prevalence of overseas production by MNEs) may result from the difficulty of agreeing licensing terms due to the information problems of the technology market (notably buyer uncertainty).

(iii) Rationalised/Specialised Operations (the efficiency-seeking MNEs)

In its pure form, import-substituting manufacturing by MNEs envisages an overseas subsidiary producing a complete product (or range of products) and selling that output to the local market. However, the most prevalent development among manufacturing MNEs in the last quarter century, by contrast, has been a move towards the rationalisation of the activity within their global network of productive facilities. This involves the specialisation of a particular subsidiary on either a small part of a much wider product range (product specialisation), or on discrete stages in the production of a particular product (process specialisation). As the complement to this there has been a growth in intra-firm but inter-country MNE trade (see Dunning, 1983, p.121).

Where the rationalised MNE predominantly emphasises product specialisation within individual subsidiaries, it may be seeking to make the optimal use of locations particularly suitable to the production of particular products, or to maximise the economies of scale in the manufacture of individual products. An important additional advantage of MNEs over potential local producers of these products (e.g. motor vehicles, electrical appliances, agricultural machinery) is an established world market for the firm's products, backed by an efficient global marketing network. Though sub-contracting may be an alternative means to achieve some of the benefits of product specialisation, MNEs often prefer to keep such activity 'in-house', both to maximise their share of the returns earned from the efficient coordination of activities, and to make the most effective use of their developed expertise in smooth global adjustment (which would be compromised by the need for frequent renegotiation of the roles of independent, but inter-linked, partners).

Process specialisation is likely to occur where the various stages involved in the production of a good require a different combination of factor inputs, so that it is desirable to locate certain unskilled labour-intensive operations in low-wage economies, and the more capital- and/or skill-intensive in the more developed industrialised countries. Of course the viability of this form of integration/specialisation requires that the cost savings *within* locations are not negated by transport costs *between* locations. Thus it has predominated in goods (consumer electronics, some instruments, such as cameras) with high value-to-transport-cost ratios. We shall elaborate more on process specialisation (in particular) when discussing intra-firm trade later (see Section 1.6).

(iv) Trade and Distribution

Many manufacturing MNEs have, in recent years, paid considerable attention to the development of their trade and distribution networks through the initiation of subsidiaries specialising in these functions. As a distinctive activity this is likely to be most visible where production characteristics (e.g. the need to reap economies of scale) lead to output being much more concentrated than markets, but where the markets may require constant and distinctive attention (i.e. close customer contact). Thus trade and distribution subsidiaries of an MNE are expected to develop markets, provide after-sales service and generally protect the company's name, in ways that contracted agents might not be guaranteed to do.

(v) Ancillary Services

Recent years have seen the extensive internationalisation of such services as insurance, banking, finance and all kinds of business consultancies (UNCTC, 1988). In some cases, the intention is to provide the services to indigenous enterprises in the overseas country; in others to follow the global expansion of leading manufacturing enterprises with which they have established relationships.

(vi) Miscellaneous Developments

Recent developments in technology (notably in air travel and information transfer) have led to significant increases in the scope of internationalisation in areas such as financial portfolio management, and internationally coordinated airline and hotel booking facilities. This may be leading to an increasing dominance of large global operations in such areas.

1.2 The Evolution of the MNE

Having indicated the wide range of activities now indulged in by the MNE, and having hinted at the complex and pervasive nature of its contemporary operations, we now turn to review briefly its early antecedents and its distinctive evolution over the last century. (For a more detailed exposition of these perspectives, related to the changing international economic, technological and political environment, see Dunning, 1983).

(i) The Early Beginnings

Prior to the industrial revolution there were several antecedents of the MNE. These include (a) chartered companies supported by their states, seeking to develop new lands and trading routes, and (b) wealthy individuals and families, usually engaged in commerce, banking and land development.

Perhaps the earliest recorded MNEs were, in fact, the Italian banking families of the Renaissance period, but their impact on home and host countries was insignificant by comparison with the chartered land and trading companies of the 16th and 17th centuries. Many colonies were exploited in this way, predominantly by UK, Dutch and French capitalists. Even at this stage, evidence of foreign manufacturing activity begins to appear among the more prominent resource-oriented operations.

Another factor contributing to an early cross-border transfer of productive assets (notably capital and skills), resulting in the setting up of industries in new locations, was substantial population migrations. However, since many such migrants effectively terminated contact with their previous homelands (especially where motivated by persecution) little of the productive capability that accompanied them can be seen as prefiguring MNE behaviour, in the form of sustained cross-border intra-enterprise connections.

(ii) The Start of the Modern MNE: 1870–1914

The exodus of capital, skills and entrepreneurship persisted with the continuing opening up of new territories and trade routes. The US began to emerge alongside the traditional investors, and throughout the 19th and early 20th centuries most FDI continued to be directed to colonial territories.

But the institutional mode of foreign activity changed dramatically with the evolution of financial and managerial capitalism, and the emergence of the joint stock company as its main organisational form. Between 1870 and 1914 we may distinguish four kinds of FDI; each, to some degree, probably represents a synthesis of existing modes of overseas activity with the pervasive influence of managerial and financial capitalism:

(a) expatriate investment by migrant capitalists, e.g. the migration of UK firms and individuals to the USA;
(b) owner-managed investment, e.g. mining in Africa and Canada;
(c) finance capitalism, e.g. European investment in Russia;
(d) trading investments, e.g. Hudson's Bay Co., Royal Africa Co.

Of these (b) and (d), in particular, hint at the type of inter-country coordination of operations from which the MNE, as now perceived, would emerge.

The motivations of these ventures were basically twofold, broadly representing the emergence of the first two types of international production listed in Section 1.1. Firstly, supply-oriented operations sought to develop primary products for the investing countries. Though many of the enterprises involved here focused on the primary stage of resource exploitation, in some industries (tobacco, oil, cocoa, asbestos) vertically integrated manufacturing firms were already involved, internalising several stages of production.

Secondly, market-oriented operations emerged to supply local markets with goods which could not be provided (or provided as cheaply) by exports from the home country. Included among these were a whole range of new consumer industries supplying branded goods (e.g. cigarettes, cocoa, margarine, chocolate, glass, preserved milk) which companies like Nestlé, Lever and Cadbury were able to take advantage of.

As Table 1.1 indicates, in 1914 the UK was the most important source country of MNEs. However the emerging strength of the US was already becoming clear; and it was pre-eminently that country which was pioneering the technological and organisational advances which were to be the hallmark of the modern MNE (see Dunning, 1983, p.86).

Table 1.1 Estimated Stock of Accumulated Foreign Direct Investment by Country of Origin, 1914–78

	1914		*1938*		*1960*		*1971*		*1978*	
	$mn	*%*	*$mn*	*%*	*$bn*	*%*	*$bn*	*%*	*$bn*	*%*
Developed countries	**14,302**	**100.0**	**26,350**	**100.0**	**66.0**	**99.0**	**168.1**	**97.7**	**380.3**	**96.8**
North America										
USA	2,652	18.5	7,300	27.7	32.8	49.2	82.8	48.1	162.7	41.4
Canada	150	1.0	700	2.7	2.5	3.8	6.5	3.8	13.6	3.5
Western Europe										
UK	6,500	45.5	10,500	39.8	10.8	16.2	23.7	13.8	50.7	12.9
W. Germany	1,500	10.5	350	1.3	0.8	1.2	7.3	4.2	28.6	7.3
France	1,750	12.2	2,500	9.5	4.1	6.1	7.3	4.2	14.9	3.8
Belgium					1.3	1.9	2.4	1.4	5.4	1.4
Italy					1.1	1.6	3.0	1.7	5.4	1.4
Netherlands	1,250	8.7	3,500	13.3	7.0	10.5	13.8	8.0	28.4	7.2
Sweden					0.4	0.6	2.4	1.4	6.0	1.5
Switzerland					2.0	3.0	9.5	5.5	27.8	7.1
Other developed countries										
Russia	300	2.1	450	1.7	—	—	—	—	—	—
Japan	20	0.1	750	2.8	0.5	0.7	4.4	2.6	26.8	6.8
Australia										
New Zealand	180	1.3	300	1.1	1.5	2.2	2.5	1.4	4.8	1.2
South Africa										
Other	Neg.	Neg.	Neg.	Neg.	1.2	1.8	2.5	1.4	5.2	1.3
Developing countries	**Neg.**	**Neg.**	**Neg.**	**Neg.**	**0.7**	**1.0**	**4.0**	**2.3**	**12.5**	**3.2**
TOTAL	14,302	100.0	26,350	100.0	66.7	100.0	172.1	100.0	392.8	100.0

Source: Dunning (1983), Table 5.1

(iii) The Inter-War Years: 1918–1939

During this period, vertical integration in primary products continued to expand (particularly in oil, rubber, tobacco and tropical fruits), but most overseas manufacturing was defensive, in response to trade barriers. These years also saw an emphasis on rationalisation and mergers (notably in the motor vehicle industry), and the introduction of new financial and organisational methods which made the management of larger firms easier. As a result, the pattern of international production became more concentrated and dominated by large firms.

(iv) The Early Post-War Period: 1939–1960

This may be seen as a crucial interim period in the development of the contemporary MNE. At the time, the most powerful factor encouraging outward direct investment from the US was the dollar shortage. While supply-oriented and market-oriented investments remained predominant, the latter was the more prominent area of growth (Dunning, 1983, p.94). Also developing in this period were bases for vital developments most strongly felt after 1960. The surge of technological advances stimulated by wartime research was building the foundations of the industries most amenable to new production methods, and also creating the technology (e.g. information transfer systems, improved freight transport) necessary to facilitate these new modes of operation. Also in this period many developing countries became politically independent, setting the scene for the cycles of conflict and reconciliation between MNEs and these host countries in the ensuing quarter century.

(v) The Later Post-War Period: 1960 to Date

In the last three decades the globally rationalised MNE has emerged, while the first two types of international production have been relatively less significant. There has also been a marked increase in all types of ancillary FDI.

Supply oriented, resource-based MNE activity has declined both as a result of improvements in some commodity markets (there is now less incentive to internalise the full vertically-integrated sequence), and due to the risk of nationalisation in some LDCs. Import-substituting manufacturing investments have expanded, but less rapidly than in the previous decade. In some cases, where technology is now standardised and mature, the MNE has been replaced by indigenous suppliers. In others, the policy re-orientation of host countries, away from import-substitution towards export-oriented industrialisation, has removed the artificial supports (protection, tax incentives) which induced local-market-oriented MNE activity in the first place.

The period also witnessed the recovery of European nations as leading outward direct investors; while the emergence of Japan and subsequently the LDCs as exporters of capital further undermined the US economic hegemony.

Some of the more important of these developments will be further discussed and documented in subsequent sections of this chapter.

1.3 The MNE in the 1980s — Some Data

To reflect the position and orientation of the MNE in the global economy in the 1980s we review two sources of data, one providing the most

Table 1.2a World Stock of Outward Direct Investment by Region

	Amount (US $mn)		*Percentage distribution*		*Percentage annual average growth*
	1975	*1983*	*1975*	*1983*	*1975/83*
All countries	280,135.6	591,572.4	100.0	100.0	9.7
Developed areas (total)	272,035.6	575,599.9	97.1	97.3	9.8
Europe	117,687.3	249,466.4	42.0	42.2	9.8
EEC	88,680.4	197,518.3	31.7	33.4	10.5
UK	37,001.7	88,543.2	13.2	15.0	19.1
Netherlands	19,922.3	39,120.9	7.1	6.6	8.8
W. Germany	14,353.8	38,934.6	5.1	6.6	13.3
France	10,607.5	17,242.3	3.8	2.9	10.2
Other Europe	29,006.9	51,948.1	10.4	8.8	7.6
Switzerland	22,442.7	40,532.2	8.0	6.9	7.7
Sweden	4,670.4	6,761.4	1.7	1.1	4.7
Norway	728.7	1,565.6	0.3	0.3	1.0
North America	134,406.2	255,757.4	48.0	43.2	8.4
USA	124,050.0	226,962.0	44.3	38.4	7.8
Canada	10,356.2	28,795.4	3.7	4.9	13.6
Other developed countries	19,942.1	70,376.1	7.1	11.9	17.1
Japan	15,941.0	61,276.0	5.7	10.4	18.3
South Africa	2,867.3	5,679.7	1.0	1.0	8.9
Developing areas (total)	8,100.0	15,972.5	2.9	2.7	6.0
Africa	n.a.s.	698.6	n.a.s.	0.1	n.a.s.
Asia and Pacific	n.a.s.	9,509.0	n.a.s.	1.6	n.a.s.
Hong Kong	n.a.s.	2,540.0	n.a.s.	0.4	n.a.s.
Latin America and Caribbean	n.a.s.	5,581.7	n.a.s.	0.9	n.a.s.
Brazil	n.a.s.	2,010.0	n.a.s.	0.3	n.a.s.

Source: Dunning and Cantwell (1987), Table B15.
Note: n.a.s. = not available separately; authors' estimates included in relevant totals.

Table 1.2b World Stock of Inward Direct Investment by Region

	Amount (US $mn)		*Percentage distribution*		*Percentage annual average growth*
	1975	*1983*	*1975*	*1983*	*1975/83*
All countries	246,667.3	540,544.8	100.0	100.0	10.3
Developed areas (total)	183,399.4	401,084.8	74.4	74.2	10.3
Europe	98,710.6	159,696.0	40.0	29.5	6.2
EEC	85,555.3	138,308.1	34.7	25.5	6.2
UK	24,490.4	52,700.3	9.9	9.7	10.1
W. Germany	23,075.2	29,587.3	9.4	5.5	3.2
Netherlands	9,812.9	16,924.5	4.0	3.1	7.1
France	9,497.3	13,426.1	3.8	2.5	4.4
Belgium	4,176.8	9,085.2	1.7	1.7	10.2
Other Europe	13,155.3	21,387.9	5.3	4.0	6.3
Switzerland	4,084.0	8,029.4	1.6	1.5	8.8
Spain	2,909.3	4,789.2	1.2	0.9	6.4
Norway	1,541.6	3,436.8	0.6	0.6	10.5
North America	64,447.7	196,985.5	26.1	36.4	15.0
USA	27,662.0	137,061.0	11.2	25.3	22.1
Canada	36,785.7	59,924.5	14.9	11.1	6.3
Other developed countries	20,241.1	44,403.3	8.2	8.2	10.3
South Africa	8,544.5	21,041.1	3.5	3.9	11.9
Australia	8,846.2	16.138.2	3.6	3.0	7.8
Developing areas (total)	63,267.9	139,460.0	25.6	25.8	10.4
Africa	19,273.6	19,271.1	7.8	3.6	-1.0
Asia and Pacific	13,039.0	28,120.8	5.3	5.2	10.1
Latin America and Caribbean	29,386.6	73,246.2	11.9	13.6	12.1
Brazil	6,890.0	23,200.0	2.8	4.3	16.4
Mexico	4,800.0	14,898.2	1.9	2.8	15.2
Middle East	650.0	16,940.0	0.3	3.1	50.3

Source: Dunning and Cantwell (1987), Table B16.

comprehensive compilation of available FDI data, the other delineating the nature of the internationalisation of the activity of the world's leading industrial enterprises.

A recently published Directory (Dunning and Cantwell, 1987) assembles data on inward and outward FDI for 80 countries. These 80 countries are estimated to account for at least 99 per cent of the outward direct investment of companies throughout the world, and between 96 and 98 per cent of the inward direct investment stake. Tables 1.2 to 1.4 in this chapter are culled from aggregations derived in the Directory.

Table 1.2 provides data on outward and inward FDI stock, by country and region, in 1975 and 1983. Ample documentation is provided for two of the most discussed phenomena of the period, viz the relative decline of the US as home country to MNEs among outward investors, alongside its rapid expansion as a recipient of FDI; and the emergence of Japan as an

Table 1.3 Indicators of the Significance of Inward and Outward Foreign Direct Capital Stock to National Economies, 1982

	Inward investment		*Outward investment*	
	Capital stock as % of GNP	*Capital stock (US $) per head*	*Capital stock as % of GNP*	*Capital stock (US $) per head*
Developed areas	5.0	483.8	7.6	792.8
Europe	5.4	445.4	9.1	874.4
EEC	5.8	639.6	8.9	953.1
France	2.8	273.1	3.6	356.1
W. Germany	4.8	521.3	6.0	651.3
UK	11.4	910.3	19.5	1,551.2
Other Europe	3.9	150.3	10.0	665.3
Switzerland	8.1	1,294.1	41.0	6,512.5
North America	5.4	705.0	7.5	971.6
Canada	19.3	2,285.3	9.6	1,118.4
USA	4.1	537.3	7.2	956.0
Other developed countries	3.0	228.4	4.9	375.5
Japan	0.4	35.1	4.7	448.6
Developing areas	8.5	87.2	0.7	5.5
Africa	17.2	69.9	1.1	10.2
Asia and Pacific	4.1	16.8	0.9	3.7
Latin America and Caribbean	11.5	195.6	0.5	8.1

Source: Dunning and Cantwell (1987), Table B6.

important overseas investor. Table 1.3 relates the inward and outward FDI stock to GNP and population, and by so doing gives some idea of the significance of international investment to various countries and regions. Table 1.4 analyses inward and outward FDI stock, for 1975 and 1982, by economic sector. This reveals another important characteristic of FDI in recent years: namely its growing orientation towards the tertiary sector, which has occurred mainly at the expense of the secondary sector.

An alternative perspective on the contemporary role of international production is provided by data on the overseas sales of the 792 largest industrial enterprises in the non-communist world in 1982 (Dunning and Pearce, 1985, Part VII). A selection of these data is set out in Tables 1.5 and 1.6. The data reveal that the overseas production plus parent exports of these leading firms accounted for 42 per cent of their total sales in 1982, and that overseas production accounts for two thirds of this total. In other words the 792 largest industrial enterprises in 1982 carried out 28 per cent of their total production outside their parent countries and exported 20 per cent of the output of their parent companies.

Table 1.4a Sectoral Distribution of Outward Foreign Direct Investment Stock, 1975 and 1982

	Primary[1]		*Secondary*[1]		*Tertiary*[1]	
	1975	*1982*	*1975*	*1982*	*1975*	*1982*
Developed areas (total)[2]	—	25.9	—	42.0	—	32.1
Developed areas (total)[3]	25.6	26.2	45.8	41.9	28.6	31.9
Europe (total)[2]	—	24.7	—	45.3	—	30.0
Europe (total)[3]	24.7	25.4	48.9	45.3	26.5	29.3
France	20.9	27.3	38.6	34.8	40.5	37.9
W. Germany	4.0	4.4	60.5	58.0	35.5	37.6
Netherlands	31.2	35.0	54.2	43.3	14.6	21.7
UK	30.2	30.7	45.8	42.9	24.0	26.4
North America	25.9	28.4	45.3	41.4	28.8	30.2
Canada	21.1	28.0	50.5	46.6	28.4	25.4
USA	26.3	28.5	44.9	40.8	28.8	30.7
Other developed countries (total)	28.6	19.3	33.7	31.9	37.7	48.8
Japan	29.4	19.2	33.6	31.9	37.0	48.9
Developing countries[4]	—	21.7	—	47.4	—	30.9
Total[2]	—	25.9	—	42.0	—	32.1
Total[3]	25.6	26.2	45.8	41.9	28.6	31.9

Source: Calculated from Dunning and Cantwell (1987), Tables B2 and B3.

Notes: 1. Percentage share of each sector in the country/area's total outward direct investment stake.

2. Includes all countries for which 1982 data are available.
3. Includes all countries for which 1975 and 1982 data are available.
4. Lack of 1975 data precluded a 1975/1982 comparison.

Reference to the data from which Tables 1.5 and 1.6 were derived permits some other aggregate-level observations. Thus, of the $3,204 billion sales of the 792 firms in 1982, overseas production accounted for approximately $900 billion and parent country exports for approximately $450 billion. Of the $900 billion overseas production it is estimated that US firms accounted for $452 billion, or 50 per cent. It is this high aggregate value of overseas production (rather than a notably high overseas production ratio) which led, at least until recent years, to the treatment of international production as pre-eminently a US phenomenon. European firms account for approximately $395 billion (44 per cent) of the overseas production, with the UK having the greatest amount, $108 billion (12 per cent), followed by France, $47 billion (5 per cent), West Germany, $44

Table 1.4b Sectoral Distribution of Inward Foreign Direct Investment Stock, 1975 and 1982

	Primary[1]		*Secondary[1]*		*Tertiary[1]*	
	1975	*1982*	*1975*	*1982*	*1975*	*1982*
Developed areas (total)[2]	—	18.7	—	43.8	—	37.5
Developed areas (total)[3]	21.3	19.7	48.9	41.6	29.8	38.7
Europe (total)[2]	—	16.5	—	50.0	—	33.5
Europe (total)[3]	14.5	17.5	55.1	48.7	30.5	33.8
France	2.6	1.6	35.7	37.0	61.7	61.4
W. Germany	0.4	0.3	66.1	55.4	33.5	44.3
UK	31.7	36.0	49.5	46.0	18.8	18.0
North America	31.0	21.5	42.1	36.4	26.9	42.1
Canada	32.7	32.7	42.8	38.8	24.5	28.5
USA	28.6	16.5	41.2	35.3	30.2	48.2
Other developed countries (total)[2]	—	13.9	—	52.9	—	33.2
Other developed countries (total)[3]	19.1	19.0	40.6	38.0	40.3	43.0
Japan	15.6	11.8	65.9	63.5	18.5	24.7
Developing areas (total)[2]	—	22.1	—	55.0	—	22.9
Developing areas (total)[3]	18.6	16.7	60.4	64.3	21.0	19.0
Africa (total)[4]	—	52.4	—	28.3	—	19.3
Asia (total)[2]	—	11.0	—	53.7	—	35.3
Asia (total)[3]	13.2	17.2	57.1	56.0	29.7	26.8
Latin America (total)[2]	—	20.6	—	57.7	—	21.7
Latin America (total)[3]	20.1	16.7	61.5	66.3	18.4	17.0
Total[2]	—	19.5	—	46.5	—	34.0
Total[3]	20.9	19.2	50.5	45.3	28.6	35.5

Source: Calculated from Dunning and Cantwell (1987), Tables B2 and B3.
Notes: 1. Percentage share of each sector in the country/area's total inward direct investment stake.
2. Includes all countries for which 1982 data are available.
3. Includes all countries for which 1975 and 1982 data are available.
4. 1975 data were not available for sufficient countries to merit a 1975/1982 comparison.

billion (5 per cent), and Switzerland, $33 billion (4 per cent). Japan accounted for an estimated overseas production of $23 billion (3 per cent) and Canada for $20 billion (2 per cent).

Turning to the parent country exports of these leading enterprises, the picture is somewhat different. Here Japan claimed the largest share, i.e. $95 billion out of the total of $450 billion, this representing 21 per cent

Table 1.5 Estimated 'Internationalisation Ratios'[1] for the Leading Industrial Enterprises[2], 1982, by country (per cent)

	Overseas production ratio[3]	*Parents' export ratio*[4]	*Overseas sales ratio*[5]	*Overseas market sourcing ratio*[6]
USA	29.5	8.2	35.3	83.6
Europe (total)	38.8	31.8	58.2	66.6
W. Germany	20.6	41.3	53.4	38.6
France	29.1	30.7	50.9	57.3
UK	41.1	19.3	52.5	78.3
Italy	18.2	24.2	38.0	47.9
Netherlands	53.6	57.8	80.4	66.6
Sweden	43.2	48.1	70.5	61.3
Switzerland	76.3	65.8	91.9	83.0
Japan	5.6	24.4	28.6	19.4
Other countries (total)	12.6	32.1	40.7	30.9
Canada	33.4	24.4	49.7	67.2
Total	28.1	19.5	42.2	66.8

Source: Dunning and Pearce (1985), Table 7.5.

Notes: 1. For information sources, and derivation of the estimates incorporated in this table, see Dunning and Pearce (1985), pp. 130–1.
2. Covers the leading 792 (non-Communist) industrial enterprises in 1982. For the derivation of this sample see Dunning and Pearce (1985), pp. 8–11.
3. Sales of overseas affiliates and associate companies (excluding goods imported from parent for resale) divided by total worldwide sales of group.
4. Parent companies' exports divided by parent companies' total sales.
5. Sales of overseas affiliates plus parent exports divided by total worldwide sales of group.
6. Sales of overseas affiliates divided by sales of overseas affiliates plus parent country exports.

Table 1.6 Estimated 'Internationalisation Ratios'[1] for the Leading Industrial Enterprises,[2] 1982, by Industry (per cent)

	Overseas production ratio[3]	*Parents' export ratio*[4]	*Overseas sales ratio*[5]	*Overseas market sourcing ratio*[6]
Aerospace	8.0	31.0	36.4	22.0
Office equipment (including computers)	32.6	15.3	42.9	76.0

Table 1.6 (continued)

Electronics and electrical appliances	23.3	26.0	43.3	53.9
Measurement, scientific and photographic equipment	23.5	30.5	46.8	50.1
Industrial and agricultural chemicals	27.9	26.1	46.7	59.8
Pharmaceuticals and consumer chemicals	41.3	11.5	48.1	85.9
Motor vehicles (incl. components)	21.8	32.0	46.8	46.5
Total High Research Intensity[7]	24.8	26.7	44.9	55.2
Industrial and farm equipment	22.8	29.9	46.0	49.8
Shipbuilding, railroad and transportation equipment	2.3	25.0	26.6	8.5
Rubber	35.0	18.2	46.8	74.7
Building materials	32.0	8.7	38.1	84.4
Metal manufacturing and products	15.2	26.2	37.4	40.7
Total Medium Research Intensity[7]	19.5	25.1	39.7	49.1
Textiles, apparel and leather goods	15.9	17.8	30.9	51.6
Paper and wood products	14.6	13.7	26.4	55.5
Publishing and printing	23.1	4.1	26.2	88.1
Food	31.9	5.2	35.5	90.0
Drink	25.2	8.2	31.3	80.5
Tobacco	44.0	7.9	48.4	90.8
Total Low Research Intensity[7]	27.9	8.5	34.1	82.0
Petroleum	38.1	11.5	45.2	84.3
Other manufacturing	20.4	15.5	32.7	62.2
Total	28.1	19.5	42.2	66.8

Source: Dunning and Pearce (1985), Table 7.6.

Notes:
1. For information sources, and derivation of the estimates incorporated in this table, see Dunning and Pearce (1985), pp. 130–1.
2. Covers the leading 792 (non-Communist) industrial enterprises in 1982. For the derivation of this sample, see Dunning and Pearce (1985), pp. 8–11.
3. Sales of overseas affiliates and associate companies (excluding goods imported from parent for resale) divided by total worldwide sales of group.
4. Parent companies' exports divided by parent companies' total sales.
5. Sales of overseas affiliates plus parent exports divided by total worldwide sales of group.
6. Sales of overseas affiliates divided by sales of overseas affiliates plus parent country exports.
7. For an explanation of these research-intensity groupings, see Dunning and Pearce (1985), p. 10.

compared with its 3 per cent share of overseas production. The USA ranks a close second with estimated parents' exports of $90 billion, though this 20 per cent share of exports is a clear contrast with its 50 per cent share of overseas production. Overall, European exports of $200 billion were 44 per cent of the sample total, West Germany clearly leading with $70 billion (16 per cent), twice the figure for France with $35 billion (8 per cent) and the UK with $30 billion (7 per cent).

From the industry point of view 'petroleum' dominates overseas production with $360 billion, or 40 per cent of the estimated 792 firm total; next come 'motor vehicles' and 'food', each with 8 per cent of the total, followed by 'electronics and electrical appliances' and 'industrial and agricultural chemicals' with 7 per cent each.

1.4 Understanding the MNE — A Theoretical Framework

Over the past two decades economists have become increasingly aware of the need to derive a general theory of international production. While various strands of economic theory (e.g. trade theory, theories of industrial location, the theory of the firm, industrial organisation) offer valuable insights into different aspects of FDI and MNE activity, a comprehensive or eclectic approach which embraces the 'why' or 'how is it possible', the 'where' and the 'how' of international production, is now generally favoured by scholars.

Perhaps the dominant paradigm which has emerged in the 1980s has been Dunning's eclectic paradigm (Dunning, 1981 and 1988). This states that there are three interrelated conditions which determine the propensity for the firms of a particular country to engage in (or increase their) overseas production. The first is the extent to which enterprises possess, or can gain privileged access to, assets which provide them with a competitive advantage over local firms in the countries in which they may operate. The literature suggests that these *ownership-specific advantages* are necessary to overcome the inherent advantages of indigenous firms in the foreign locations in which MNEs operate (e.g. a greater knowledge of local labour markets, the capability of suppliers, the needs of customers and expertise in dealing with the local bureaucracy). The second condition is whether these enterprises find it appropriate to use such advantages themselves (i.e. to internalise the markets for them) or whether they choose to isolate and sell them (or their rights) to other firms for them to use by way of licensing, management contracts, franchising, etc. The extent to which firms prefer the hierarchical or the market route depends on the relative transactions costs of the two organisational modalities. The third condition is whether or not the firms choose to locate at least part of the production generated by their ownership advantages in overseas locations, rather than meet any foreign demand by exports. The possible *location-specific advantages* influencing this decision include input and transport costs, comparative productivity, and government policies including those affecting trade.

It is argued that changes in the configuration of ownership-location-internalisation (OLI) advantages provide coherent explanations for the rise, persistence or decline of the various types of international production identified in Section 1.1, and for the progressive evolution of MNE forms and modes of operation outlined in Section 1.2. Let us illustrate with reference to the use of rationalised international production, of the process-specialisation sort. *Location factors* are clearly fundamental here. The MNE discerns a number of overseas locations with distinctive characteristics (e.g. labour supply, available raw materials, types of host-government support) such that the spread of the various stages of its production process across these various locations (i.e. process specialisation in particular countries) will enhance its competitive position in cost terms.

The possession of *ownership advantages* by MNEs, *vis-à-vis* independent local firms, can be considered almost axiomatic in the procedure under discussion, when it is recalled that their activity in any particular country is only a specialised part of the MNE's wider technology. Nevertheless, if we exclude independent local suppliers (using their own technology) in a particular country as potential intruders into the MNE's integrated network, the possibility of sub-contracting local firms (with a complementary transfer of relevant technology) as an alternative to owned affiliates can be considered. Where such sub-contracting does not occur, and the MNE retains a fully integrated network of owned affiliates, certain *internalisation advantages* will have prevailed. These may include (i) the desire to protect the value of highly rated technology or managerial assets, and not to risk their dissipation or abuse through sub-contractors, (ii) the desire to keep the greatest possible control over quality at each stage, and to minimise the risk of disruption due to sub-standard (or delayed) output at particular locations, (iii) the need to retain the maximum degree of flexibility in the system, which might be compromised by the interjection of independent suppliers, and (iv) the desire to maximise the returns to a particular asset, where an exceptional expertise in global coordination of operations has emerged as a distinctive characteristic of the MNE's management.

In illustrative summary, then, the eclectic theory suggests that an individual foreign subsidiary in a process-specialisation MNE network exists, because the MNE *owns* relevant productive assets not available to local firms, because the host country has *locational* assets less favourably available to the MNE elsewhere, and because the MNE perceives reasons to keep the operations performed by the facility fully *internal* to its own network.

1.5 Evaluating the MNE — A Framework of Issues

As would be expected with an institution which has grown and evolved so rapidly in recent decades, numerous frictions and controversies have grown up around the MNE. Rather than cataloguing these frictions and controversies we propose that progress towards articulating the dimensions of a particular debate may be facilitated by the delineation of three *types* of issue which may underlie any evaluation of the MNE. These issues relate to (a) efficiency, (b) distribution, (c) sovereignty and self-reliance. Of course, any particular area of debate may embody elements of two or more of these issue-types, but it is contended that the ability to discern such distinctive components within a controversy will contribute towards, at least, a better definition of the differences to be resolved.

Many of the controversies relating to the MNE, including some referred to by way of illustration below, have their most visible and virulent manifestation when they concern Less Developed Host Countries (LDCs). This reflects the facts that (a) MNEs' ownership-advantages are likely to differ from the capabilities of indigenous LDC enterprises much more than from those of indigenous enterprises in other industrialised countries, and (b) the location-advantages offered by LDCs are likely to be very distinctively different from those in the MNE's home country, or other industrialised countries. As we shall indicate, whereas these characteristics may provoke serious *distribution* conflicts between MNEs and LDCs, they also present considerable opportunities for *efficiency* gains.

Efficiency of Resource Allocation

The issue of efficiency is essentially concerned with the extent to which there exist complementarities of economic interest between MNEs and host countries. More specifically, the following paragraphs address the question: 'Under what conditions do the operations of an MNE affiliate in a host country contribute to raising world economic welfare to a level that could not have been achieved in any other way?'

Of course, the establishment and survival of MNE affiliates in foreign countries does not itself *prove* the existence of efficiency in the terms we have defined it. It is well known that the foreign expansion of firms may be based upon imperfections, including the generally oligopolistic market structure in which they seek to maximise returns from their advantages, and also the imperfections in factor markets which limit the ability of host countries to seek the 'unpackaging' of the MNE. At the same time the presence of MNE operations in certain host countries, notably LDCs, is often prompted by government-induced imperfections or distortions, such as protection against imports or the dualistic structure of the host economy. In such cases, far from advancing efficiency, the activities of MNEs may create a high-income elite market for capital-intensive production, which might work against both the comparative advantage of the LDC and optimal resource allocation within the MNE.

In fact, this type of import-substituting (usually high-technology) investment is described by Kojima (1978) as 'trade destroying', since the local production replaces trade that would have occurred under the dictates of comparative advantage. More appropriate, according to Kojima, is investment in LDCs in which the ownership advantages of the MNE (knowledge, management, etc.) are complementary with the undistorted location advantages of the LDC (e.g. cheap labour, mineral resources, etc.). Such MNE involvement, it is argued, allows the LDC to realise its dynamic comparative advantage, and will thus be 'trade creating'. Kojima suggests that this latter type of FDI was typified by the early post-war wave of Japanese investment in its poorer Asian neighbours. Thus the suggestion of the Kojima thesis is that in such industries as motor vehicles, consumer electronics, textiles and apparel, Japanese firms had a long-standing competitive advantage based on a mastery of a relatively standardised technology which they used in conjunction with well-motivated and low-cost labour in Japan. However, while Japanese *firms* retained these ownership advantages (e.g. technology, management expertise, design and marketing skills and established world-wide marketing networks), Japanese *production* diminished in competitiveness as wage rates (a crucial location factor in these industries) rose. The Japanese firms were then motivated to move their production overseas in search of cheap labour. In this scenario the benefits of FDI would be widely spread. The Japanese firms are able to retain their competitive edge, which implies that their customers also gain, while the host countries realise their economic potential with increased employment and foreign exchange gains through exports. Though Kojima's theory has been disputed (Buckley, 1983 and 1985), and empirical studies do not wholly support it (for a survey see Casson and Pearce, 1987a, pp. 113–4), we have presented the argument in some detail here as a useful indication of efficiency elements in a prominent line of argument.

Distribution

Here we are concerned with how the gains (or losses) that accrue from MNE operations in host countries are divided between the partners. From the viewpoint of the host countries it is not enough to show that MNEs contribute to a growth in world economic welfare that could not otherwise have been achieved. No less important to the recipients of FDI is the desire to obtain what they consider to be a fair share in the benefits created by the investment.

Clearly the identification of a *fair* distribution of the surplus created by MNE operations is a very difficult task, as it involves the 'appropriate' pricing of factors of production such as technology, management, etc. This becomes even more contentious when the profitability of an MNE project is due less to the efficiency with which resources are allocated, and more to market distortions and imperfections created, or sustained, by host governments. Under such circumstances the distribution of economic rent would almost inevitably be strongly influenced by the relative bargaining strength of MNEs and the host government, with conditions such as tax concessions, tariff protection for final products, tariff concessions on imported inputs, labour training and export targets being negotiated.

However, even if we accept that the concept of an entirely just distribution of the benefits of FDI is a difficult one to deal with, this does not alter the fact that, in many countries which are host to the affiliates of MNEs, there is real concern lest the host country, through ignorance or inadequate bargaining power, is not able to extract that share of the benefits it believes it should.

Two reasons would be advanced for this view:

(a) Imperfections in the markets for the factors of production in which MNEs are strong allow them to earn monopoly rents on these factors.
(b) Partially related to (a) is the view that, when distribution is strongly dependent on bilateral bargaining between MNEs and, especially, LDC governments, the MNE is in the stronger position. For elaboration on this contention, and a survey of empirical studies of MNE-LDC bargaining, see Casson and Pearce (1987a, pp. 121–3).

Clearly, in discussing this issue of distribution, the most obvious conflict of interests is that between the foreign enterprise and the indigenous economy. However, a slightly different perspective may prove instructive. This derives from the view that MNE activity, notably in LDCs, often creates an enclave which is largely isolated from the rest of the economy. This criticism was originally directed against FDI in the extractive and plantation sectors; in the 1970s it has been increasingly raised against some capital-intensive manufacturing sectors. It is alleged, for example, that sectors such as consumer electronics employ a small high-income elite of local labour which then develops consumption patterns based on imported goods, or the output of the foreign firms in the enclave. Obviously, if the indigenous components of these enclaves are included with the foreign firms in a distribution analysis, these would be likely to obtain the vast majority of the benefits, with little spillover of benefits into the traditional sector of the local economy.

Two points are emphasised in this case:

(a) In considering the distributional consequences of FDI it would be wrong to neglect income distribution effects *within* the host country (see Dunning, 1981, p. 16). It is, for example, possible for a host country to gain a satisfactory share of the economic rents generated by the MNE, while at the same time its internal income distribution is worsened.
(b) Amongst the benefits which MNEs may generate (especially in LDC host countries) are spillovers and spread-effects, increasing the economic viability of indigenous industry and distributing income growth more widely.

Sovereignty and Self-Reliance

However favourably an MNE may be evaluated by a particular host country on purely economic criteria, it seems almost inevitable that its foreignness *per se* will, to some degree, be viewed with concern. Thus all countries, to varying degrees, place a value on independence. The areas of debate subsumed here under the heading of sovereignty and self-reliance derive from the ways in which the MNE might compromise (or perhaps enhance) the economic independence of host countries in the short and longer term.

Here we may consider the issues relating to *economic sovereignty* to be short-term ones, relating to ways in which the behaviour of MNEs may compromise the effectiveness of certain areas of host country policy. The general flexibility and power of MNEs, and in particular the manifestation of these in the form of intra-group resource transfers, are often alleged to undermine the autonomy of host countries in areas such as fiscal policy, monetary policy, trade policy and attempts to organise or control the structure of industry.

The areas of discussion, which we categorise as *self-reliance*, concern ways in which the operations of MNEs in host countries may either undermine the viability of independent indigenous enterprise or enhance its potential. One facet (see Casson and Pearce, 1987a, pp. 107–8) concerns the effects of MNEs on the industrial structure of host countries, e.g. with respect to levels of concentration and modes of competition. On the one hand, it is asserted that MNEs might promote a more efficient competitive structure by increasing the number of firms, breaking up monopolies and cartels, and by inducing indigenous firms to embrace new practices and technology. On the other hand, it is contended that MNEs may reduce competition by out-competing local firms, fairly or unfairly (e.g. by subsidised predatory pricing), and securing monopoly positions for themselves. Increased concentration may also result if local firms feel stimulated to merge in order to compete effectively with MNE entrants. This kind of theorising on the likely effects of MNEs on host country industrial structure tends to assume that MNE affiliates and local firms are substitutes for each other, in the sense of competing for the same market. Equally, however, it is possible that the relationship between MNE subsidiaries and local firms may be one of complementarity, which may reflect matching technical specialisations of the firms, or factors relating to the optimal use of capacity. Thus vertical linkages may be established between foreign and local firms, which may generate spillover benefits for the rest of the economy (see Casson and Pearce, 1987a, pp. 108–10). Such sub-contracting relationships might benefit local firms, either by providing them with an additional outlet for their existing products, or by contributing to a general upgrading of their productive capability.

1.6 Rationalised MNE Production and Intra-Firm Trade

The prevalence of intra-firm trade conducted within MNEs may be seen as a way in which they use a particular expertise to achieve *efficiency* by optimally dispersing productive operations, or as one of the crucial instruments that these institutions may use to distort the *distribution* of the benefits to which they contribute (and thus subvert the economic *sovereignty* of host countries).

Earlier we referred to the emergence of rationalised production by MNEs, and the linking of geographically dispersed operations, as providing the rationale for the high levels of intra-firm trade. In this section we present brief documentation of the phenomenon of such trade and discuss the forms of product or process specialisation which underlie it.

Data for 1982, compiled by the US Department of Commerce (see Casson and Pearce, 1987b, Tables 7 and 8), show that 82.8 per cent of US foreign affiliates' exports to the US were intra-group (i.e. to the parent or other US-based affiliates), while 38.8 per cent of US foreign affiliates' exports to other non-US locations were intra-group. For manufacturing affiliates the comparable ratios were 86.1 per cent (to US) and 58.4 per cent (to rest of world). Similarly, in 1982, 84.0 per cent of US overseas affiliates' imports from the US were intra-group (i.e. from the parent or other US-based affiliate), with the comparable figure for manufacturing being 83.1 per cent. Table 1.7, based on analysis of a sample of the world's leading enterprises in 1982, suggests that, though the US may have led the way in promoting rationalised production and intra-group trade, other countries also have a substantial commitment to it, especially in high-

Table 1.7 Internal Exports Ratio[1], for Leading Firms[2], by Area and Industry, 1982 (per cent)

	USA	*Europe*	*UK*	*Other, incl. Japan*	*Total*
Aerospace	0.5	9.5	n.a.s.		3.2
Office equipment (including computers)	75.5	75.1		n.a.s.	71.9
Electronics and electrical appliances	18.5	32.1	18.3	35.1	28.1
Measurement, scientific and photographic equipment	78.3	n.a.s.			78.1
Industrial and agricultural chemicals	31.6	26.9	48.9	14.6	27.7
Pharmaceuticals and consumer chemicals	80.2	50.4	45.2	36.8	60.2
Motor vehicles (including components)	94.9	62.5	n.a.s.	5.2	60.5
Total High Research Intensity	47.1	44.2	40.4	17.1	42.6
Industrial and farm equipment	66.3	42.0	25.2	23.4	46.1
Building materials	30.1	4.5	7.6	6.3	7.9
Metal manufacturing and products	10.3	18.2	19.6	77.4	20.7
Total Medium Research Intensity	40.6	18.9	18.2	23.9	23.1
Textiles, apparel and leather goods	0	17.8	17.3	2.2	7.9
Paper and wood products	0.8	2.9		0	1.7
Publishing and printing	14.9	28.0			21.6
Food	12.5	35.6	19.2	8.0	30.3
Drink		13.7	11.3		13.7
Total Low Research Intensity	4.9	19.3	13.9	2.7	13.2
Petroleum	35.3	4.8	n.a.s.	0	17.4
Other manufacturing	10.0	n.a.s.	n.a.s.	11.0	5.8
Total	43.1	33.2	24.8	15.5	34.0

Source: Dunning and Pearce (1985), Table 7.7.

Notes: n.a.s. = results not given for reasons of confidentiality and disclosure. The information is, however, included in the appropriate aggregates.

1. Proportion of parent's total exports accounted for by exports to overseas affiliates.
2. Covers the 172 firms, from the 792-firm sample described in section 1.3, for which data on 'internal exports' were available.

technology industries. The dominance of intra-group trade in most of these latter sectors is primarily attributable to the desire of firms in these sectors to keep control over (i.e. to internalise) the technological and marketing advantages they have created for themselves. Thus in such industries, with innovative products, there is a strong incentive for the parent company to produce the most sophisticated components itself and supply them predominantly to wholly-owned overseas subsidiaries (see Casson and Pearce, 1987b).

Perhaps the most prominent example of the emergence of rationalised MNE activity of the product-specialisation type can be found in the response of US MNEs to the setting up of the EEC (see Dunning, 1983, p. 131). To capture the economies of scale and centralisation of production, but to take advantage of a free trade area, firms which were previously truncated replicas of their parent companies, each producing a similar range of products for individual national markets without trade, found it economic to specialise in particular products for all markets in the region, and to trade these products across national boundaries.

Though a substantial amount of intra-firm trade generated by process-specialisation takes place between developed countries (see Casson and Pearce, 1987b), perhaps the most distinctive form of this behaviour is that involving 'export platform investment' in LDCs. This type of investment occurs in technologically quite advanced industries, but at those points on the value-added chain which require labour-intensive methods. The procedure is that firms locate this stage of production in LDCs, while other stages of production in the vertically integrated production process are located in the developed countries, where the final product is usually sold. The reason for this is obviously to perform the labour-intensive stages of production in countries where the real cost of labour is the lowest. The predominant form that the procedure takes is to import a capital intensive intermediate product into an LDC, have the labour-intensive process performed on it there, and re-export it back to the parent country, either as a finished good or for further stages in processing. In industries such as electronics the motivation for the setting up of such offshore plants, by US MNEs in particular, may be seen as defensive. Thus the sectors of the industry which adopted this type of activity most strongly appear to have been those most vulnerable to price-competitive imports, and thus most in need of new sources of low cost inputs.

Many goods are amenable to rationalised production, among the most familiar being electrical appliances and machinery, machine tools, motor vehicle components and precision instruments. The essential characteristics needed for the process to be viable are (a) that it does have a labour-intensive stage which, (with value added) accounts for a reasonably large part of the final value of the product, and (b) that the good has a sufficiently high value-to-transport-cost ratio, to avoid transport costs cancelling out the production cost savings. Also, if the goods can be economically transported by air, the flexibility gained may save on inventory costs.

This 'export platform' type of process-specialisation by MNEs is facilitated by institutional factors on both the parent-country and host-country sides. The principal facilitating factor on the parent-country side is tariff provisions which allow goods involved in such a process to be assessed for duty, on re-entry into the parent country, only on the value added overseas and not on the full value of the goods as imported (see, for example, US tariff schedules 806.30 and 807.00).

On the host-country side many LDCs have made positive efforts to encourage the growth of such processing stages within their economies. The most prevalent form of encouragement has been the setting up of Export Processing Zones (EPZs). These are specially designated industrial areas or estates which (a) allow all imports (including capital goods) and exports to be free of tariff or other trade restrictions, (b) incorporate all the necessary infrastructure, factories, port or airport facilities, and (c) offer special packages of financial inducements, including, for example, tax holidays, low tax rates and the hire of factory space at concessional rents. (For further documentation and evaluation of EPZs, see Casson and Pearce, 1987a, pp. 110–12).

Since the offshore assembly operations discussed above are usually in industries which are subject to continual technological evolution, any particular operation of this type may be vulnerable to quite short-term obsolescence. Indeed, technological advances in the design and computerisation of manufacturing processes may have reversed the tendency to use this mode in recent years. Most notably there has been a drastic reduction in the number of parts incorporated into such products as TV sets, motor vehicles and video recorders, a fall in the labour-cost component of these products, and a growing advantage in having the different stages of production along a value-added chain located in the same place. Examples of divestment by MNEs in South-East Asia include the relocation by Philips of its TV chassis assembly to Western Europe in 1985, and by RCA of the assembly of its surveillance camera from Taiwan to Pennsylvania. When Apple produced its first mini-computer the assembly of its components was undertaken in Singapore and Malaysia, and the final assembly performed in Texas. However, for the second generation of computer the entire product is produced in a highly-automated assembly plant in California, which operates on a one-shift basis where direct labour costs represent less than 3 per cent of total costs (UNCTC, 1988).

1.7 Conclusion

In this chapter we have traced various aspects of the evolution of the MNE and distinguished some of its contemporary characteristics. We have also attempted to set out, and illustrate, a framework for analysing and evaluating the MNE. A persistent theme of the chapter has been the ability of the MNE to benefit from the common governance of a group of geographically dispersed activities, which are linked together by a substantial amount of intra-group trade. It should be clear that optimal use of such behaviour by MNEs, and its control by national governments, places a great priority on the derivation and use of adequate techniques of financial reporting.

References

Buckley, P.J. (1983) 'Macroeconomic versus international business approach to direct foreign investment: a comment on Professor Kojima's interpretation', *Hitotsubashi Journal of Economics*, 24, pp. 97–100.

Buckley, P.J. (1985) 'The economic analysis of the multinational enterprise: Reading versus Japan', *Hitotsubashi Journal of Economics*, 26, pp. 117–24.

Casson, M.C. and Pearce, R.D. (1987a) 'Multinational enterprises in LDCs' in N. Gemmell (ed.) *Surveys in Development Economics*, Basil Blackwell.

Casson, M.C. and Pearce, R.D. (1987b) 'Intra-firm trade and the developing countries', in D. Greenaway (ed.) *Economic Development and International Trade*, Macmillan.

Dunning, J.H. (1981) *International Production and the Multinational Enterprise*, Allen and Unwin.

Dunning, J.H. (1983) 'Changes in the level and structure of international production: the last one hundred years', in M.C. Casson (ed.) *The Growth of International Business*, Allen and Unwin.

Dunning, J.H. (1988) *Explaining International Production*, Allen and Unwin.

Dunning, J.H. and Cantwell, J. (1987) *IRM Directory of Statistics of International Investment and Production*, Macmillan Reference Books.

Dunning, J.H. and Pearce, R.D. (1985) *The World's Largest Industrial Enterprises, 1962–1983*, Gower.

International Monetary Fund (1977) *Balance of Payments Manual*, Fourth Edition, IMF, Washington.

Kojima, K. (1978) *Direct Foreign Investment — A Japanese Model of Multinational Business Operations*, Croom Helm.

Pearce, R.D. (1987) 'Host countries and the R & D of multinationals: issues and evidence', *University of Reading Discussion Papers in International Investment and Business Studies*, No. 101.

UNCTC (1988) *Transnational Corporations in World Development: Fourth Survey*, United Nations, New York.

Further Reading

Buckley, P.J. and Casson, M.C. (1985) *The Economic Theory of the Multinational Enterprise*, Macmillan.

Caves, R.E. (1982) *Multinational Enterprise and Economic Analysis*, Cambridge University Press.

Dunning, J.H. and Archer, H. (1987) 'The eclectic paradigm and the growth of UK multinational enterprises, 1870–1983', *University of Reading Discussion Papers in International Investment and Business Studies*, No. 109.

Hood, N. and Young, S. (1979) *The Economics of Multinational Enterprise*, Longman.

Part II
COMPARATIVE FINANCIAL REPORTING

2
The Causes of Financial Reporting Differences

CHRISTOPHER W. NOBES

2.1 Introduction

That there are major international differences in financial reporting practices is not obvious to all accountants, let alone to non-accountants. The latter may see accounting as synonymous with double entry, which is indeed fairly similar universally. This chapter investigates the major differences between some countries in much more detail. As a prelude to this, it is instructive to try to identify the likely causes of the differences. It is not possible to be *sure* that the factors discussed below cause the financial reporting differences, but a relationship can be established and reasonable deductions made.

There seems to be consensus, on the whole, about which factors are involved in shaping financial reporting. Some researchers have used their estimates of such causes as a means of differentiating between countries (Mueller, 1967). Other researchers have studied whether perceived differences in accounting practices correlate with perceived causal factors (Frank, 1979). Factors which are seen as influencing accounting development include the nature of the legal system, the prevalent providers of finance, the influence of taxation, and the strength of the accountancy profession (Nobes and Parker, 1985, Ch. 1).

On a world-wide scale, factors like language or geography have been referred to by the above-mentioned researchers. To the extent that these do have some explanatory power, it seems more sensible to assume that this results from auto-correlation. That is, the fact that Australian accounting bears a marked resemblance to accounting in New Zealand might be 'confirmed' by language and geographical factors. However, most of their similarities were probably not *caused* by these factors, but by their historical connection with the UK, which passed on both accounting and language, and was colonising most parts of Australasia in the same period.

If one wanted to encompass countries outside the developed western world, it would be necessary to include factors concerning the state of development of their economy and the nature of their political economy. Of course, to some extent a precise definition of terms might make it clear that it is impossible to include some of these countries. For example, if our interest is in the financial reporting practices of listed corporations, those countries with few or no such corporations will have to be excluded. Fortunately, as our main purpose concerns multinationals and their base countries, there is a reasonable degree of uniformity in such countries concerning the presence of developed economies, democratic governments, listed companies, qualified accountants, and so on. For our purposes, the following seven factors may constitute an explanation for financial reporting differences: legal systems, providers of finance, taxation, the accounting profession, inflation, theory, and the accidents of history.

2.2 Legal Systems

Some countries have a legal system which relies upon a limited amount of statute law, which is then interpreted by courts, which build up large amounts of case law to supplement the statutes. Such a 'common law' system was formed in England primarily by post-Conquest judges acting on the king's behalf. It is less abstract than codified law (see below); a common law rule seeks to provide an answer to a specific case rather than to formulate a general rule for the future. Although this common law system emanates from England, it may be found in similar forms in many countries influenced by England. Thus, the federal law of the USA, the laws of Ireland, India, Australia, and so on, are to a greater or lesser extent modelled on English common law. This naturally influences company law, which traditionally does not prescribe a large number of detailed, all-embracing rules to cover the behaviour of companies and how they should publish their financial statements. To a large extent (at least up until the 1981 Companies Act in the UK), accounting within such a context is not dependent upon law.

Other countries have a system of law which is based on the Roman *jus civile* as compiled by Justinian in the sixth century and developed by European universities from the twelfth century. Here rules are linked to ideas of justice and morality; they become doctrine. The word 'codified' may be associated with such a system. This difference has the important effect that company law or commercial codes need to establish rules in detail for accounting and financial reporting. For example, in West Germany, company accounting is to a large extent a branch of company law. Both the nature of regulation and the type of detailed rules to be found in a country are affected.

Table 2.1 illustrates the way in which developed countries' legal systems fall into these two categories. In some countries, *dirigisme* is compounded with centralisation and a desire to control the economy, and this results in the existence of an 'accounting plan' (see Chapter 3).

Table 2.1 Western Legal Systems

Common Law	*Codified Roman Law*
England and Wales	France
Ireland	Italy
	W. Germany
	Spain
United States	Netherlands
Canada	Portugal
Australia	
New Zealand	Japan (commercial)

Note: The laws of Scotland, Israel, South Africa, Quebec, Louisiana and the Philippines embody elements of both systems.

2.3 Providers of Finance

The prevalent types of business organisation and ownership also differ. In France and Italy, capital provided by the state or by banks is very significant, as are small family businesses. In West Germany, the banks in particular are important owners of companies as well as providers of debt finance. A majority of shares in some public companies are owned or controlled as proxies by banks, particularly by the Deutsche, Dresdner and Commerz banks. In such countries the banks or the state will, in many cases, nominate directors and thus be able to obtain information and affect decisions. If it is the case that many companies in continental countries are dominated by banks, governments or families, the need for *published* information is less clear. This also applies to audit, because this is designed to check up on the managers in cases where the owners are 'outsiders'.

Evidence that this characterisation is reasonable may be found by looking at the number of listed companies in various countries. Table 2.2 shows the numbers of domestic listed companies on Stock Exchanges where there are over 250 such companies. The comparison between the UK and West Germany or France is instructive. A two-group categorisation of these countries is almost as obvious as that for legal systems in Table 2.1 (taking account of size of economy or population). Incidentally, the country with the longest history of 'public' companies is the Netherlands. Although it has a fairly small stock exchange, many multinationals (such as Unilever, Philips, Royal Dutch) are listed on it. It seems reasonable, then, to place the Netherlands with the English-

Table 2.2 Stock Exchanges with over 250 Domestic Company Shares, 1986

Exchange	*Companies*
America	747
Australia	1,162
Amsterdam	267
Barcelona	324
Copenhagen	274
W. Germany	492
Johannesburg	536
Korea	355
London	2,101
Luxembourg	253
Madrid	312
Montreal	622
New York	1,516
New Zealand	339
Osaka	1,050
Paris	482
Rio de Janeiro	658
Sao Paulo	592
Tel Aviv	255
Tokyo	1,499
Toronto	1,034

Source: Fédération Internationale des Bourses de Valeurs, Annual Report, 1986.

Table 2.3 Institutional Shareholdings: Percentage of Equities held by Institutions

Year	*UK*	*USA*
1963	26	23
1969	37	—
1975	52	34
1978	49	—
1980	60	41

Source: Sibley (1981), pp. 118, 119.

speaking world in a 'shareholder' group as opposed to a 'bank/state/family' group.

Although it is increasingly the case that shares in countries like the UK (and the USA) are held by institutional investors rather than by individual shareholders (see Table 2.3), this still contrasts with state, bank or family holdings. Indeed, the increased importance of institutional investors is perhaps a reinforcement for the following hypothesis:

> In countries with a widespread ownership of companies by shareholders who do not have access to internal information there will be a pressure for disclosure, audit and 'fair' information.

Institutional investors hold larger blocks of shares and may be better organised than private shareholders. So, they should increase this pressure, although they may also be able successfully to press for more detailed information than is generally available to the public.

'Fair' needs to be defined. It is a concept related to that large number of outside owners who require unbiased information about the success of a business and its state of affairs (Stamp, 1980 and Flint, 1982). Although reasonable prudence will be expected, these shareholders are interested in comparing one year with another and one company with another; thus the accruals concept and some degree of realism will be required. This entails judgement, which entails experts. This expertise is also required for the checking of the financial statements by auditors. In countries like the UK, the USA and the Netherlands, this can, over many decades, result in a tendency to require accountants to work out their own technical rules. This is acceptable to governments because of the influence and expertise of the accounting profession, which is usually running ahead of the interest of the government (in its capacity as shareholder, protector of the public interest or collector of taxation). Thus 'generally accepted accounting principles' control accounting. To the extent that governments intervene, they impose disclosure, filing or measurement requirements and those tend to follow best practice rather than create it.

In most continental European countries, the traditional paucity of 'outsider' shareholders has meant that external financial reporting has been largely invented for the purposes of governments, as tax collectors or controllers of the economy. This has not encouraged the development of flexibility, judgement, fairness or experimentation.

Nevertheless, even in such countries as Germany, France or Italy, where there are comparatively few listed companies, governments have recognised the responsibility to require public or listed companies to publish detailed, audited, financial statements. There are laws to this effect in the majority of such countries, and in France and Italy the government has also set up bodies specifically to control the securities markets: in France the *Commission des Opérations de Bourse* (COB), and in Italy the *Commissione Nazionale per le Società e la Borsa* (CONSOB). These bodies are to some extent modelled on the Securities and Exchange Commission (SEC) of the USA (See Section 2.8). They have been associated with important developments in financial reporting, generally in the direction of Anglo-American practice. This is not surprising, as these stock exchange bodies are taking the part otherwise played by private and institutional shareholders who have, over a much longer period, helped to shape Anglo-American accounting systems.

In France the COB was formed in 1968. Its officers are appointed by the government. It is charged with encouraging the growth of the Bourse by improving the quality of published information and the operations of the market. It has established listing requirements and has investigated cases of non-compliance with publication and disclosure requirements. Perhaps its most obvious campaign has been to introduce consolidation. In 1968, consolidation was extremely rare, even for listed companies. Matters improved substantially under pressure from the COB, including a requirement to consolidate for all companies wishing to obtain a new listing. This is discussed further in Chapter 3.

Although there are far fewer listed companies in Italy than there are in France (Italy does not even figure in Table 2.2), the effect of the CONSOB may be even greater than that of the COB, partly because of the much less satisfactory state of affairs in Italy before the CONSOB's formation in June 1974. Because Italy is not dealt with at any length in Nobes and Parker (1985) some further details are given here. The CONSOB has powers to call for consolidation or extra disclosures but it has not used these powers extensively yet. However, its real influence is linked to the Presidential Decree No. 126 of March 1975 which, after much delay, was introduced by statutory instrument. This requires listed companies to have a more extensive audit, undertaken by an auditing company approved by the CONSOB. This requirement is in addition to the statutory audit by *sindaci*, or state registered auditors. Its introduction has been phased, with the largest listed companies complying by 1982, followed by smaller listed companies and banks. As a rule, the new audits have been carried out initially by the only accountants experienced in this sort of work, that is, the international auditing firms. The scope of the audit includes checking that the books are properly kept and up to date, and that the accounts are in accordance with the books, the civil code and 'generally accepted accounting principles'. Because the requirements of the fiscal law are still strong in some cases, such as bad debt provisions and depreciation, there are many instances where the international firms are not able to sign 'fairly present' statements, but may still sign 'legal' and 'clear' and disclose the differences from 'fair'.

In order to strengthen the hand of the new auditors, the Italian professional body, the *Ordine dei Dottori Commercialisti*, has set up a committee to issue accounting and auditing principles (*principi contabili* and *prinicipi di revisione*). These principles – issued in 1979 – are advisory for listed companies and others. The committee contains representatives from international firms, and the accounting principles bear considerable resemblance to Anglo-American practice and thus to the standards of the International Accounting Standards Committee. Further, partly because the Commercial Code is widely drawn, there are no substantial inconsistencies between the Code and the new principles. There are, of course, differences between the principles and the fiscal laws. This problem has yet to be fully resolved. However, it is clear that the government, the CONSOB and the *Ordine* are in favour of practices similar to Anglo-American accounting.

In 1981 the government itself issued obligatory accounting principles for use by the many state-controlled companies, some of which are very large. Again, advice was sought from international firms and the resulting principles, though different in some respects from the *principi contabili* of the *Ordine*, represent a significant shift towards 'fair' accounting.

The effects of all this on the accounting of state and listed companies could well be revolutionary. The backing by government and the CONSOB of accounting principles has weakened the hand of tax inspectors, who had previously established the scope of 'tax accounting' well beyond (and against) the requirements of the Commercial Code. This process was started by the tax reforms of 1974, and has also been reinforced by findings of the commercial court, the *Tribunale di Milano*, in favour, for example, of depreciation based on the Commercial Code rather than on tax laws.

All this change creates a problem for the process of classification of Italian accounting among the systems of other countries. The culmination of the changes may be expected by 1990, but some of the effects discussed above have been occurring gradually over the years since 1974. There are more details on Italian accounting in Chapter 3.

2.4 Taxation

Although it is possible to make groupings of tax systems in a number of ways, only some of them are of relevance to financial reporting. For example, it is easy to divide EEC countries into those using 'classical' and those using 'imputation' systems of corporation tax (Nobes, 1985). However, this distinction does not affect financial reporting. What is much more relevant is the degree to which taxation regulations determine accounting measurements. To some extent this is seen in a negative way by studying the problem of deferred taxation, which is caused by timing differences between tax and accounting treatments. In the UK, the Netherlands and the USA, for example, the problem of deferred tax has caused much controversy and a considerable amount of accounting standard documentation.

Turning to France or West Germany, it is found that the problem does not really exist; for in these countries it is to a large extent the case that the tax rules *are* the accounting rules. In West Germany, the commercial accounts (*Handelsbilanz*) should be the same as the tax accounts

(*Steuerbilanz*). There is even a word for this idea: the *Massgeblichkeitsprinzip* (the principle of bindingness!).

One obvious example of the areas affected by this difference is depreciation. In the UK, the amount of depreciation charged in the published financial statements is determined according to custom established over the last century and influenced by the accounting standard SSAP 12. The standard points out that:

> Depreciation should be allocated to accounting periods so as to charge a fair proportion of the cost or valuation of the asset to each accounting period expected to benefit from its use . . . (para 1) . . . Management should select the method regarded as most appropriate to the type of asset and its use in the business so as to allocate depreciation as fairly as possible . . . (para 8).

The injunctions contained in the standard are of a fairly general nature, and their spirit is quite frequently ignored. Convention and pragmatism, rather than exact rules or even the spirit of the standard, also determine the method of judging the scrap value and the expected length of life (Nobes, 1985).

The amount of depreciation for tax purposes in the UK is quite independent of these figures. It is determined by capital allowances, which are a formalised scheme of tax depreciation allowances designed to standardise the amounts allowed and to act as investment incentives. Because of the separation of the two schemes there can be a complete lack of subjectivity in tax allowances, but full room for judgement in financial depreciation charges.

At the opposite extreme, in countries like West Germany, the tax regulations lay down depreciation rates to be used for particular assets. These are generally based on the expected useful lives of assets. However, in some cases, accelerated depreciation allowances are available: for example, for industries producing energy-saving or anti-pollution products or for those operating in West Berlin or other areas bordering East Germany. If these allowances are to be claimed for tax purposes (which would normally be sensible), they must be charged in the financial accounts. Thus, the charge against profit would be said by a UK accountant not to be 'fair', even though it could certainly be 'correct' or 'legal'. This influence is felt even in the details of the choice of method of depreciation, as shown by an extract from the 1986 Annual Report of AEG Telefunken (p. 23):

> Plant and machinery are depreciated over a useful life of ten years on a declining-balance basis; straight-line depreciation is adopted as soon as this results in a higher charge.

A second example of the overriding effect of taxation on accounting measurement is the valuation of fixed assets in France. During the inflationary 1970s and before, French companies were allowed to revalue assets. However, this would have entailed extra taxation due to the increase in the post-revaluation balance sheet total compared to the previous year's. Consequently, except in the special case of merger by *fusion*, when tax-exempt revaluation is allowed, revaluation was not practised. However, the Finance Acts of 1978 and 1979 made revaluation obligatory for listed companies and for those which solicit funds from the public; it is optional for others (van Waardenburg, 1979). The purpose was to show balance sheets more realistically. The revaluation was performed by use of government indices relating to 31 December, 1976. The credit went to an undistributable revaluation reserve. As a result of this, for depreciable assets, an amount equal to the extra depreciation due to revaluation is *credited* each year to profit and loss and *debited* to the revaluation account. Thus the effect of revaluation on profit (*and tax*) is neutralised. This move from no revaluations to compulsory revaluations is due to the change in tax rules.

Further examples are easy to find: bad debt provisions (determined by tax laws in many continental countries), development and maintenance expenditures (carried forward for tax purposes in Spain), or various provisions related to specific industries (see Section 3.4).

The effects of all this are to reduce the room for operation of the accruals convention (which is the driving force behind such practices as depreciation) and to reduce 'fairness'. Until the legislation following the EEC's fourth Directive, the importance of this effect was not disclosed in published accounts. With some variations, this *Massgeblichkeitsprinzip* operates in West Germany, France, Belgium, Italy, Spain and many other countries. It is perhaps due partly to the persuasive influence of codification in law, and partly to the predominance of taxation as a cause of accounting.

The alternative approach, exemplified above by the UK, the USA and the Netherlands, is found in countries with an older tradition of published accounting, where commercial rules have come first. Most of the countries on the left in Table 2.1 are, in varying degrees, like this. In most cases, there is not the degree of separation between tax and financial reporting that is found in the UK in the shape of capital allowances. However, in all such countries the taxation authorities have to adjust the commercial accounts for their own purposes, after exerting only minor influence directly on them. There is a major exception to this in the use of LIFO inventory valuation in the US, largely for tax reasons (see Nobes and Parker, 1985, Ch. 2).

2.5 The Profession

The strength, size and competence of the accountancy profession in a country may follow to a large extent from the various factors outlined above and from the type of financial reporting they have helped to produce. For example, the lack of a substantial body of private shareholders and public companies in some countries means that the need for auditors is much smaller than it is in the UK or the USA. However, the nature of the profession also feeds back into the type of accounting that is practised and *could* be practised. For example, as has been mentioned, the 1975 Decree in Italy (not brought into effect until the 1980s), requiring listed companies to have extended audits similar to those operated in the UK and the USA, could only be brought into effect initially because of the substantial presence of international accounting firms. This constitutes a considerable obstacle to any attempts at significant and deep harmonisation of accounting between some countries. The need for extra auditors was a controversial issue in West Germany's implementation of the EEC's fourth Directive (Nobes, 1986).

The scale of the difference is illustrated in Table 2.4, which lists the bodies whose members may audit the accounts of companies (but see below for explanation of the French and German situation). These remarkable figures need some interpretation. For example, let us more carefully compare the West German and the British figures. In West Germany, there is a separate, though overlapping, profession of tax experts (*Steuerberater*), which is larger than the accountancy body. However, in the UK the 'accountants' figure is especially inflated by the inclusion of many who specialise in or occasionally practise in tax. Secondly, a West German accountant may only be a member of the *Institut* if he is in practice, whereas at least half of the British figure represents members in commerce, industry, government, education, and so on. Thirdly, the training period is much longer in West Germany than it is in the UK. It normally involves a four-year relevant degree course, six years' practical experience (four in the profession), and a professional examination consisting of oral and written tests plus a thesis. This tends to last until the aspiring accountant is thirty to thirty-five years old. Thus, many of the West German 'students' would be counted as part of the qualified figure if they were in the British system.

These three factors help to explain the differences. However, there is still a very substantial residual difference which results from the much larger number of companies to be audited and the different process of forming a judgement on the 'fair' view. The differences are diminishing as auditing is extended to many private companies in EEC countries (Nobes, 1986).

Table 2.4 Age and Size of Public Accountancy Bodies

Country	*Body*	*Founding date**	*Approx. number ('000) 1987/88*
United States	American Institute of Certified Public Accountants	1887	264
Canada	Canadian Institute of Chartered Accountants	1902 (1880)	44
United Kingdom	Institute of Chartered Accountants in England and Wales	1880 (1870)	87
	Institute of Chartered Accountants of Scotland	1951 (1854)	12
	Chartered Association of Certified Accountants	1939 (1891)	30
	Institute of Chartered Accountants in Ireland	1888	6
Australia	Australian Society of Accountants	1952 (1887)	55
	Institute of Chartered Accountants in Australia	1928 (1886)	17
New Zealand	New Zealand Society of Accountants	1909 (1894)	15
Netherlands	*Nederlands Instituut van Registeraccountants*	1895	6
France	*Ordre des Experts Comptables et des Comptables Agréés*	1942	11
West Germany	*Institut der Wirtschaftsprüfer*	1932	5
Japan	Japanese Institute of Certified Public Accountants	1948	10

Note: * Dates of earliest predecessor bodies in brackets.

It is interesting to note a further division along Anglo-American versus Franco-German lines. In the former countries, governments or government agencies do require certain types of companies to be audited, and put certain limits on who shall be auditors, with government departments having the final say. However, in general, membership of the private professional accountancy bodies is the method of qualifying as an auditor. On the other hand, in France and West Germany there is a dual set of accountancy bodies. Those in Table 2.4 are not the bodies to which one

Table 2.5 Accountancy Bodies in France and West Germany

	Private professional body	*State auditing body*
France	*Ordre des Experts Comptables*	*Compagnie Nationale des Commissaires aux Comptes*
West Germany	*Institut der Wirtschaftsprüfer*	*Wirtschaftsprüferkammer*

must belong to qualify as an auditor of companies, though to a large extent the membership of these professional bodies overlaps with that of the auditing bodies, and membership of the former permits membership of the latter. The auditing bodies are shown in Table 2.5. The professional bodies set exams, consider ethical matters, belong to the international accounting bodies, and so on. The auditing bodies are run by the state. The *Compagnie Nationale* is responsible to the Ministry of Justice; the *Wirtschaftsprüferkammer* to the Federal Minister of Economics.

2.6 Inflation

Although accountants in the English-speaking world have proved remarkably immune to inflation when it comes to decisive action, there are some countries where inflation has been overwhelming. In several South American countries, the most obvious feature of accounting practices is the use of methods of general price-level adjustment (Tweedie and Whittington, 1984; Nobes and Parker, 1985, Ch. 11). The use of this comparatively simple method is probably due to the reasonable correlation of inflation with any particular specific price changes when the former is in hundreds of per cent per year; to the objective nature of government published indices; and to the paucity of well-trained accountants.

Without reference to this factor, it would not be possible to explain accounting differences in several countries severely affected by it.

2.7 Theory

In a few cases, accounting theory has strongly influenced accounting practice, perhaps most obviously in the case of microeconomics in the Netherlands. Accounting theorists there (notably Theodore Limperg, Jr) had advanced the case that the users of financial statements would be given the fairest view of the performance and state of affairs of an individual company by allowing accountants to use judgement, in the context of that particular company, to select and present accounting figures. In particular, it was suggested that replacement cost information might give the best picture. The looseness of law and tax requirements, and the receptiveness of the profession to microeconomic ideas (partly due, no doubt, to their training by the academic theorists) has led to the present diversity of practice, the emphasis on 'fairness' through judgement, and the experimentation with and practice of replacement cost accounting.

2.8 Accidents

Many other influences have been at work in shaping accounting practices. Some are not indirect and subtle like the type of ownership of companies, but direct and external to accounting like the framing of a law in response to economic or political events. For example, the economic crisis in the USA in the late 1920s and early 1930s produced the Securities and Exchange Acts which have diverted US accounting from its previous course by introducing extensive disclosure requirements and control (usually by threat only) of accounting standards. Other examples include the introduction into Italy of Anglo-American accounting principles by choice of the government, and the introduction into Luxembourg of consolidation and detailed disclosure as a result of EEC Directives – both against all previous trends there. In Spain, the 'artificial' adoption of the accounting plan from France follows the latter country's adoption of it after influence by the occupying Germans in the early 1940s. Perhaps most obvious and least natural is the adoption of various British Companies Acts or International Accounting Standards by developing countries with a negligible number of the sort of public companies or private shareholders which have given rise to the financial reporting practices contained in these laws or standards. In its turn, the UK in 1981 adopted uniform formats derived from the 1965 *Aktiengesetz* of West Germany because of EEC requirements. For their part, Roman Law countries are now having to grapple with the 'true and fair view' (see Section 3.1).

2.9 Summary and Conclusion

This chapter has discussed some of the influences on the development of financial reporting practices. The importance of the mix of users of accounting information seems clear; it has a major part to play in the emergence of the dominant source of rules for accounting practice. In many continental European countries, the importance of governments as collectors of taxation or controllers of the economy has led to the dominance of company law, commercial codes and tax regulations. In other countries, the effective control of financial reporting practice has been exercised by the accountancy profession. This was first seen as a vague corpus of 'best' or 'accepted' practices, and has since been refined in the publication of detailed accounting standards. However, these standards are still loosely drawn documents which permit considerable flexibility and the use of judgement. The interests of private shareholders as users of financial statements have been a continuing background pressure on the profession as it develops standard practice.

As a result of international harmonisation, much of it directly caused by the EEC, many European countries are finding 'fairness' and audit thrust upon them; and the UK, Ireland and the Netherlands are receiving many detailed financial reporting rules into their laws. This development cuts across the fundamental causes of differences that we have been looking at. However, it was certainly the case, at least before this influence was widely felt, that the same countries were generally found together under most of the factors discussed above. This observation leads on to the thought of classification of countries (Nobes and Parker, 1985, Ch. 12). At this point we might note that an interesting exception to the otherwise clear pattern of countries is the Netherlands. Although, the Netherlands has a Roman legal system and few listed companies, if one studies its commercial/maritime history it bears considerable similarities to England's. Also, although the number of listed companies is small, some of those companies are very large and are the basis of an active stock exchange. At any rate, when it comes to taxation and the profession, the Netherlands appears to fit fairly well with the UK, Ireland or the USA as opposed to the continental European group.

References

Flint, D. (1982) *A True and Fair View*, Gee.

Frank, W.G. (1979) 'An empirical analysis of international accounting principles', *Journal of Accounting Research*, Autumn.

Mueller, G.G. (1967) *International Accounting*, Part I, Macmillan.

Nobes, C.W. (1985) *Depreciation Problems in the Context of Historic Cost Accounting*, Certified Accountants Research Bulletin, No. 12.

Nobes, C.W. (1986) 'New Laws for Old', *Accountancy*, December.

Nobes, C.W. and Parker, R.H. (1985) *Comparative International Accounting*, 2nd edn, Philip Allan.

Sibley, S. (1981) 'Equity ownership: the sprats and dolphins', *Accountant's Magazine*, September.

Stamp, E. (1980) *Corporate Reporting: Its Future Evolution*, Canadian Institute of Chartered Accountants, Toronto.

Tweedie, D.P. and Whittingon, G. (1984) *The Debate of Inflation Accounting*, Cambridge University Press.

van Waardenburg, D.A. (1979) 'France: the Finance Law, 1979', *European Taxation*, No. 4.

Further Reading

Choi, F.D.S. and Mueller, G.G. (1984) *International Accounting*, Chapters 1 and 2, Prentice-Hall.

3

Major International Differences in Financial Reporting

CHRISTOPHER W. NOBES

To some extent, differences in financial reporting have already been discussed in Chapter 2. This applies particularly to the first two headings below, which are therefore dealt with briefly here. Also, it should be noted that many factors overlap. For example, a discussion of conservatism tends to overlap with discussions of the accruals convention or of fairness, because the former tends to drive out the others.

It should be stated here that the intention of this chapter is not primarily to examine detailed accounting practices country by country; that is done elsewhere (e.g. Nobes and Parker, 1985, Chapters 2–7).

3.1 Fairness

The degree to which accountants and auditors search for 'fairness' as opposed to correctness or legality has differed substantially across countries. This has been discussed in Chapter 2 and has been linked to (i) a predominance of outside shareholders as providers of finance, and (ii) the lack of interference of law or taxation in financial reporting.

Until the 1980s, the laws of the UK, Ireland and the Netherlands were alone in the EEC in requiring fairness or faithfulness from audited financial statements (see Nobes and Parker, 1985, Chapters 3 and 6). On the one hand this elevates judgement of particular circumstances above uniform rules, but on the other hand it can be a far more onerous requirement for directors and auditors (as the disturbing trend of litigations illustrates; see, for example, Minnis and Nobes, 1985). It can, of course, also lead to the abuse of flexibility by directors because of the vagueness of 'fair'.

The requirement of the EEC's fourth Directive that 'true and fair' should override detailed rules in all member states may lead to a mask of uniformity that conceals the unchanged old differences. For example, the requirement that from 1 January 1984 French financial statements should give an *image fidèle* involves changes in the law and in audit reports, but French accounting seems little altered. This may make matters *worse* for Anglo-Saxon readers of financial statements, who may be misled by the increased superficial similarities.

A related concept is 'substance over form', an expression usually associated with the USA. In an attempt to 'present fairly', US accountants have come to the view that it is necessary to try to account for the economic substance of events rather than for the legal form. For example, it is deemed necessary to capitalise assets obtained on finance leases as though they had been bought (SFAS 13) and it is necessary to record interest 'paid' or 'received' at reasonable rates even if the amounts actually involved are substantially larger or smaller (APB Opinion 21). This approach has also given rise to a UK accounting standard (SSAP 21) along similar lines to SFAS 13.

It should also be said that there is a subtle transatlantic difference in the concept of fairness. In the EEC, fairness is now an overriding concept; in the US, it is necessary to 'present fairly in accordance with generally accepted accounting principles'. It is not clear what would happen in a case of conflict.

A concern with fairness also lies behind the Dutch experimentation and use of replacement cost valuation, and the agonised attempts in the English-speaking world since the late 1960s to replace or supplement historical cost accounting.

In great contrast to all this is the example of West Germany where, until 1987 financial statements, there was still no preference for fairness over rules, or for substance over form. Financial reporting is still an exercise in accurate bookkeeping which must satisfy detailed rules and the scrutiny of the tax inspector. The recent requirement for French and German accounts to be 'fair' has largely been met by extra disclosures rather than a change in the presentation of numbers in the financial statements.

3.2 Taxation

The influence of taxation has been discussed in Chapter 2 as a cause of differences in financial reporting. In most continental European countries, it is one of the enemies of fairness. In its effects on depreciation, bad debt provisions and some asset valuations it is a major example of differences in financial reporting.

3.3 Conservatism and Accruals

Another traditional adversary of fairness is conservatism. Perhaps because of the different mix of users in different countries, conservatism is of differing strength. For example, the importance of banks in West Germany may be a reason for greater conservatism in reporting. It is widely held that bankers are more interested in 'rock-bottom' figures in order to satisfy themselves that long-term loans are safe. At the same time, the consequent lack of interest in a 'fair' view reduces the importance of the accruals convention which would normally modify conservatism.

In the UK it is now more usual to refer to the concept of 'prudence' (as in SSAP 2 and now in company law). In many cases, accounting standards are the compromise treaties which settle a battle between conservatism and the accruals concept. For example, it is not fully conservative to allow the capitalisation of development expenditure as in SSAP 13, but it may be reasonably prudent under certain conditions. A similar argument applies to the taking of profit on long-term contracts as in SSAP 9. Many other Anglo-Saxon countries use similar ideas, although US accounting practice does not go far. For example, it does not allow capitalisation of development expenditure (SFAS 1).

Continental European conservatism is of a more stringent variety, as may be illustrated by a study of published accounts. The annual report of *AEG Telefunken* 1986 will be examined here. The evidence of conservatism in such reports depends upon the events of the year and the style of the companies' reports, thus it is not possible to organise a consistent survey. However, this report seems to be broadly representative of the practice of listed companies in West Germany and is only presented as an example of the type of evidence available. The quotations below come from page 25 of the report and are designed to give an impression of the conservatism. Reports of other years would provide similar quotations.

> *Inventories:*
> Raw materials . . . are valued at the lower of cost and a lower value, to the extent that it is economically required or permissible.
> Full provision has been made for anticipated losses. . . Write downs for slow-moving and obsolete inventories are taken to cover all anticipated risks.
>
> *Debtors:*
> Receivables have been valued after providing for all known risks. . . In addition, the collection risk is covered in a general allowance for doubtful debts.
>
> *Sundry provisions:*
> All anticipated risks are taken into account in the valuation of other accrued expenses.

> *Foreign debt:*
> Liabilities in foreign currencies [are held] at the higher of the exchange rate at the time of acquisition or at year end.
>
> *Depreciation:* (from an earlier year's report)
> Special provisions have been made where there are risks due to economic factors and obsolescence.

As a postscript, it may be noted that investment analysts greatly increase a West German company's profit figures by a series of adjustments before comparing them to a UK figure (Beeny, 1975, Chapter 4; Occasional Papers on Earnings per Share by *Deutsche Vereinigung für Finanzanalyse und Anlageberatung*). However, matters have 'improved' somewhat since the 1965 *Aktiengesetz*. Before that, it was suggested (Semler, 1962) that

> If the non-existence of a contingency cannot be absolutely determined, then in the interest of protecting the creditor it must be assumed that such a contingency exists.

This greater conservatism in continental Europe seems to be a long-run phenomenon. Davidson and Kohlmeier (1966) and Abel (1969) noted that profit figures would be consistently lower in France, Sweden, West Germany and the Netherlands (when use of replacement cost was assumed) if similar companies' accounts were merely adjusted for differences in inventory and depreciation practices from those used in the USA or the UK. Gray (1980) examined France, West Germany and the UK in order to produce an index of conservatism. He concluded that 'French and German companies are significantly more conservative or pessimistic than UK companies' (p. 69).

A further example of the protection of creditors is the use of statutory or legal reserves in several continental countries. These are undistributable reserves that are set up out of declared profits. They are an extra protection for creditors above the normal Anglo-American maintenance of capital rules. In France, West Germany and Italy a company is required to appropriate 5 per cent tranches of its annual profit until the statutory reserve reaches 10 per cent of issued share capital (20 per cent in Italy).

A particular piece of evidence of the lack of importance of the accruals concept (though not of conservatism) in West Germany is the absence of a 'provision for proposed dividends' in annual balance sheets. Since there needs to be an AGM to bring the dividends into legal existence, they cannot exist at the balance sheet date! French balance sheets compromise between the German and the UK view by presenting the liabilities and capital side of a balance sheet in two columns: before and after allocation of net profits.

There are some more remarks concerning conservatism and accruals in Section 3.4.

3.4 Provisions and Reserves

The distinction between provisions and reserves is important for financial reporting because the former are charges against profit, whereas the latter are appropriations of profit. The influences which lead to a proliferation of significant provisions appear to be conservatism and rigid but generous tax regulations. Both these factors have been discussed, and their effects on provisions mentioned. The result of such provision accounting may be that the accruals convention and 'fairness' are partially overriden; this in turn may result in income smoothing.

The use of accelerated depreciation in the financial accounts is an example of over-provision. The lack of provision for bad debts in a system where it is not allowed for tax purposes is an example of under-provision. Provisions for risks and contingencies which fluctuate in reverse relationship with profits are examples of income smoothing. This may be illustrated using annual reports of the French and West German companies referred to above and in Chapter 2.

In the 1983 Annual Report of Total Oil (CFP), there is a Chartered Accountants' Report (p. A5) which notes that in the UK 'the provision for contingencies would be classified as a reserve'. In earlier years, there were even more revealing remarks in the versions of the annual reports of CFP that were specially prepared for UK readers:

> Depreciation of property, plant and equipment was F. 2,274 million compared with F. 2,283 million in 1976. Provision amounts were lower in 1977 than in 1976, especially because cash flow reflected on the French market did not allow constitution of a provision for foreign exchange fluctuations at the same level as in 1976 (1977, p. 22).
>
> Taking into account these items, income for the year was F. 111 million, to which must be added a deduction of F. 90 million from the 'Provision for contingencies'. Income finally amounts to F. 201 million (F. 237 million in 1976) but includes lower exceptional income (1977, p. 23).
>
> Following the usual effect of amounts set aside to or written back from depreciation and provisions and an allocation of F. 800 million to reconstitute the provision for contingencies, net income for the year totalled F. 971 million (F. 266 million in 1978) (1979, p. 23).

A useful comparison may also be made between the treatment of provisions in the statutory (parent company) accounts and their treatment as reserves in consolidated accounts which have been influenced by Anglo-Saxon practices (and auditors). This is clearer in earlier years, before fiscal revaluation in the 1978 accounts. As a result of the 1983 Law requiring fairness, CFP transferred its contingency 'provision' to 'reserves' in 1984.

With reference to West Germany, remarks concerning provisions have already been made in the section on conservatism. One further brief

Table 3.1 Worldwide Consolidated Profit and Loss Account of *AEG Telefunken* for the Years 1985 and 1986 (DM '000)

		1986	*1985*
Sales	**11,220,320**		**10,842,882**
Increase of inventories of finished and semi-finished goods and contracts in process	+ 59,105		+ 83,033
		11,279,425	10,925,915
Capitalised cost of own production of fixed assets		+ 77,373	+ 71,123
Total operating performance		**11,356,798**	**10,997,038**
Cost of raw materials, supplies and merchandise		– 5,212,304	– 5,153,816
Gross profit		**6,144,494**	**5,843,222**
Income from profit and loss transfer agreements	2,561		2,310
Income from investments in subsidiaries and affiliated companies	13,472		19,585
Income from other financial assets	974		577
Other interest and similar income	102,537		161,921
Gain from disposals of fixed assets and financial assets and, in 1986, from revaluation of fixed assets	55,038		8,308
Gain from release of accrued expenses	27,262		42,848
Gain from release of special untaxed reserves	1,185		3,686
Miscellaneous income	380,045		409,953
of which extraordinary income: 4,569			(32,844)
		+ 583,074	+ 649,188
		6,727,568	6,492,410
Salaries and wages	3,500,075		3,250,829
Social security expenses	591,882		556,012
Expenses related to pensions and support payments			

Pension payments	109,382		101,021
Additions to pension accruals	284,846		138,206
	394,228		239,227
Voluntary support payments	2,927		2,781
	397,155		242,008
Depreciation of fixed assets	295,080		315,935
Depreciation of investments in subsidiaries and affiliated companies	79		—
Losses from reduction in value or disposals of current assets (other than inventories), and addition to general allowance for doubtful accounts	50,921		71,754
Losses on disposals of fixed assets and financial assets	9,189		8,858
Interest and similar expenses	101,057		197,635
Taxes			
on income and net worth	55,192		46,029
other	15,961		28,139
	71,153		74,168
Losses under profit and loss transfer agreements	13,792		17,598
Additions to special untaxed reserves	3,684		1,342
Miscellaneous expenses	1,693,501		1,756,271
		− 6,727,568	− 6,492,410
Net income		—	—
Adjustment of differences and reserves arising from consolidation		− 12,495	− 16,874
		− 12,495	− 16,874
Minority interest in earnings	− 3,776		− 4,549
Minority interest in losses	+ 16,271		+ 21,423
		+ 12,495	+ 16,874
Unappropriated consolidated retained earnings		—	—

quotation will suffice to show a parallel with French practices quoted above; it comes from the Report of *AEG Telefunken*, 1978:

> Provisions for pensions . . . have remained unchanged as compared to the previous year . . . To hold the cover at the previous year's level of 80% would have required an additional provision of DM 58 million.

In the 1986 profit and loss account, it may be seen in Table 3.1 that the 'consolidated result' is exactly zero for 1985 and 1986! The adjustments in the last few lines are presumably not discretionary (as they deal with consolidation adjustments and minority interests); so the inevitable conclusion must be that the 'loss/profit for the year' is a figure arrived at by working backwards from the 'consolidated result' of zero. This is income smoothing on a heroic scale.

It appears that in Italy and Spain the Commercial Codes (which would certainly allow greater use of the accruals convention) have been overriden to a large extent by the need to satisfy the requirements of tax inspectors. Only recently, and particularly in Italy, have tax reforms and stronger accounting principles allowed the use of 'fairer' provisions of various types.

In the UK, provisions for depreciation and bad debts are not supposed to be affected by tax requirements. Provisions for risks and contingencies are rare and usually associated with cases where a liability is fairly certain in incidence, if not in amount. Broadly speaking, these practices prevail in the rest of the English-speaking world and in the Netherlands. However, there is an important exception in the treatment of deferred tax, which is fully provided for in the USA, Canada, Australia and the Netherlands, but (since the late 1970s) not in the UK.

3.5 Valuation Bases

There is great international variation in the predominant basis of valuation and the degree to which there is experimentation and supplementation with alternative measures. In a country with detailed legal rules and a coincidence of tax and commercial accounting it must be expected that the predominant valuation system will be the one that involves as little judgement as possible. Flexibility and judgement would make it difficult for auditors to determine whether the law had been obeyed and might lead to arbitrary taxation demands. Thus, in a country such as West Germany, it seems unsurprising that the required method of valuation is a strict form of historical cost. This has extended to the use of book values rather than fair values for the consolidation of subsidiaries' assets (see Section 3.6 below).

At the other extreme is the Netherlands. Some Dutch companies (e.g. Philips) have published replacement cost financial statements since the early 1950s. Although this remains minority practice, many Dutch companies partially or supplementarily use replacement costs. Dutch practice reflects the influence of microeconomic theory and a striving after fairness.

In between these two extremes, UK 'rules' allow a chaotic state of affairs where some companies revalue, some of the time, using a variety of methods. Also, there has been experimentation with current cost accounting, normally as supplementary statements. This is the story for most of the English-speaking world, except that the USA and Canada keep to historical cost in the main financial statements; this is because of the influence of the SEC.

In France, Spain and Italy, where there is much tax and other government influence, there has also been more inflation than in Germany and a great drive towards the creation of large and efficient equity capital markets. Governments and stock exchange bodies in these countries have appreciated the effects of inflation on historical cost accounting and have required revaluations. However, this creates severe problems in such countries. France will be used as an example here.

In Chapter 2 the matter of the fiscal revaluation in France in 1978 was discussed. Because of the link with taxation and law, and because of an absence of a strong and innovatory body of accountants, revaluation had to be done uniformly or not at all. Thus, French revaluation was done compulsorily, all at once, and using government indices. It was tax-exempt and has led to subsequent annual depreciation adjustments for tax purposes. This process is sufficiently ungainly that it has not happened since 1978, and it is now of negligible benefit because the resulting figures are neither cost nor current.

Many countries, notably in South America, have adopted forms of general purchasing power (GPP) adjusted accounting. This has occurred in countries with very high inflation, government/tax controlled accounting, and a paucity of accountants. Thus GPP satisfies the requirements of simplicity and uniformity, as a single inflation index can be used by all companies. GPP accounting is of course basically historical cost accounting with 'last minute' annual indexations.

3.6 Consolidation

The prevalence of consolidation has varied dramatically among EEC countries. Most practices seem to have first enjoyed widespread adoption in the USA: for example, the normal acquisition method, the equity method and the pooling of interests/merger method. There are examples of consolidation at least as far back as the 1890s, and it was universal practice by the early 1920s (Walker, 1978; Hein, 1978). The various factors that might have caused this early development in the USA may help to explain the diversity in the EEC. The US factors may have been:

(i) a wave of mergers at the turn of the century, leading to the carrying on of business by groups of companies;
(ii) the prevalence of the holding company (which merely owns investments) as opposed to the parent company (which is one of the operating companies of the group);
(iii) the lack of a legal requirement for holding/parent company balance sheets, unlike the UK law, for example;
(iv) the lack of legal or other barriers to the emergence of new techniques, and the existence of innovative professionals;
(v) the use of consolidation for tax purposes (1917 to 1934);
(vi) acceptance of consolidation by the New York Stock Exchange (1919).

In the UK consolidation came later. Holding companies were perhaps less important until World War I, although there was a UK wave of mergers at the turn of the century (Payne, 1967). Nevertheless, UK mergers did not usually involve holding companies. Also, tax computations never moved to a consolidated basis in the UK. It used to be commonly held that Nobel Industries (ICI) pioneered consolidation in the early 1920s (e.g. Walker, 1978, p. 25) and Dunlop in the 1930s. However, Edwards and Webb (1984) have found much earlier evidence. The latter researchers also suggest that UK managements were opposed to consolidated accounts, particularly because there would be less room for secret reserves and income-smoothing. The 1928 Act (consolidated in 1929) contained no consolidation requirements (the Greene Committee had received some evidence 'for' from the Law Society but 'against' from the Institute of Chartered Accountants in England and Wales!); the Stock Exchange required consolidation as a condition of new issues from 1939.

However, in the UK, consolidated financial statements were seen as supplements to parent company balance sheets, whereas they were seen as substitutes in the USA. This may be because of the greater importance of holding companies and the lack of requirements for parent/holding company accounts in the USA. In the UK consolidation grew up as a device to show investments in more detail than at cost, particularly as private subsidiaries (even of public groups) were exempt from publication requirements.

In the Netherlands, consolidation was also practised by the 1930s. However, in most of continental Europe, consolidation is either a recent development or still very rare. In Germany, consolidation was made obligatory by the 1965 *Aktiengesetz* for public companies. However, foreign subsidiaries did not need to be (and generally were not) consolidated, and the use of the equity method for associated companies was not allowed. Further, there were important differences from Anglo-American practice in the use of an economic (rather than a legal) basis for 'the group', and a yearly calculation of 'differences arising on consolidation' based on book values rather than a once-for-all calculation of goodwill based on fair values. West Germany implemented the seventh Directive in 1985, thus removing most of these differences (Nobes, 1986).

In France, before 1985, there was no law on consolidation. Thus, consolidation had been very rare. However, the formation of COB in the late 1960s and the influence of Anglo-American practices, due to the presence of international firms and the desire of some French companies for listings on the Exchanges of London or New York, caused a gradual increase in consolidation by listed companies. Naturally, in a country where there is no tradition of professional accounting measurement standards, in cases where there were no law or tax requirements, practice has been very varied. The *Conseil National de la Comptabilité*, a government body with responsibility for the *Plan*, issued guidelines in 1968 and 1978 as follows: global consolidation should be used for holdings of over 50 per cent or where full control is exercised; *mise en équivalence* (similar to equity method) for holdings of over 33⅓ per cent and at a lower level if judged appropriate; proportional consolidation for joint ventures held by two or more groups and not by the public. However, these guidelines have not been followed exactly (Nobes and Parker, 1985, Ch. 4). In 1985, a law was passed to require listed companies to publish consolidated financial statements. Other companies must follow by 1990.

In Belgium and Spain, until the 1980s, consolidation was very rare. In Italy, the CONSOB has been encouraging consolidation, but it has been rare even for listed companies. The result of lack of consolidation in these many EEC countries is that outside investors or lenders (particularly foreigners) have grossly inadequate information, even about large listed groups.

Why have most continental European countries been so far behind the UK and the USA in the development of consolidation? The reasons may include:

(i) the existence of many legal requirements that made the preparation of individual company balance sheets compulsory and militated against new ideas;
(ii) the lack of a large or strong profession to innovate;
(iii) the lesser importance of 'big business' and holding companies;
(iv) the importance of bankers and creditors who might oppose consolidation on the grounds that it confuses legal liabilities;
(v) the importance (as users of accounts) of the revenue authorities, and in some cases governments, who prefer to do their own manipulations of the accounts of individual companies;
(vi) the relative lack of importance of shareholders who may want an overall 'economic' view.

One of the effects of this rarity of consolidation was that the EEC's major draft law on financial reporting (the fourth Directive) was adopted in 1978 without any recognition of group accounting. Presumably, when the first draft was published in 1971, a requirement to consolidate would have been hopelessly controversial. This has led to what UK accountants may regard as significant curiosities in the fourth Directive (as enacted in the UK as the 1981 Companies Act); for example, the prescribed formats are not designed for use by groups and there are no requirements or rules for consolidation.

However, as we have seen, the stock exchange bodies and governments of most EEC countries have begun to take actions to require listed or public companies to consolidate. This is designed to make their domestic capital markets more efficient and to internationalise the flows of capital. It is of course logical to direct the consolidation rules at those companies where outside providers of finance are important. In addition, the seventh Directive of the EEC (first published in draft in 1976, and adopted in 1983) requires consolidation rules by 1990 (see Ch. 5).

3.7 Uniformity and Accounting Plans

The degree to which financial reporting is uniform among companies within a country varies. Before the early 1980s, when the EEC's harmonising measures began to take effect, the variations were greater. Uniformity can exist in three main areas; formats of financial statements, accounting principles and disclosure requirements. Clearly, where there are detailed legal rules in any or all of these areas, there will be a high degree of uniformity.

In order to examine the emergence of uniformity, one should probably start with Germany. It was for internal, cost accounting purposes that uniform formats were first developed. It appears that the first comprehensive chart of accounts was published in Germany by J.F. Schaer in 1911. Such charts were used by industry in the First World War. In 1927, Schmalenbach published *Der Kontenrahmen*, which was followed by the publication of model charts for different industries (Forrester, 1977). Under the National Socialists, the ascendant ideology of controlling the economy led naturally to the compulsory adoption of charts of accounts, particularly as the price mechanism was not operating due to controls on prices and money, and thus some alternative allocation mechanism was needed (Singer, 1943).

In France, the needs of the Economics Ministry, in its role as controller of the French economy, were seen to be well served by the use of accounting plans introduced by the occupying German forces in the early 1940s. Consequently, such a system has been in use in France throughout the post-war years (Most, 1971). The first full version of the *plan comptable général* was produced in 1947, and revised versions were issued in 1957 and (as partial implementation of the fourth Directive) in 1982. The *plan* exists in many versions for different industries. It comprises a chart of accounts, definitions of terms, model financial statements and rules for measurement and valuation. Thus its influence is all-pervasive. The chart must be completed each year for national statistical purposes; tax returns are based on the plan; published financial statements use the model formats; and all the former use the standard definitions and measurement rules. The *plan* even stretches to cost and management accounting.

Its use for central statistical purposes is very obvious. A government economist in Paris can collect charts for all companies and add together all amounts under a particular decimalised code in order to find the total investment in a particular type of fixed asset, defined in a standardised way. Naturally, as the government is historically the main user of accounting information in its capacities as economic controller, tax collector and provider of state capital, the *plan* is controlled by a government body: the *Conseil National de la Comptabilité*.

In Belgium, part of the process of preparing for the implementation of the fourth Directive during the 1970s was the introduction of an accounting plan in 1976, not dissimilar from the French one. The Belgians had used a chart of accounts for some industries during the inter-war years, and had experienced full use of it during the early 1940s. The *plan comptable minimum normalisé* is now compulsory. However, unlike the French *plan*, the Belgian one mainly concerns charts of accounts, which are to be sent to the *Banque Nationale*.

In Spain, an accounting plan has been progressively introduced. The Ministry of Public Finance established the Institute of Accounting Planning in 1973 which has produced several versions of the plan for different sectors. As in France, the plan consists of a chart of accounts, a set of definitions, formats for annual accounts and valuation principles. The headings of the decimalised chart of accounts are in the same order as the French chart, though the sub-headings vary to some extent. The plan began by being voluntary; then, by an Act of December 1973, the plan had to be used for those companies who wished to revalue. This continued for the 1978 and 1979 fiscal revaluations (somewhat like the French revaluations of similar date). However, by an Order of 14 January, 1980, companies covered by plans already in issue must now comply with the plans (Donaghy and Laidler, 1982).

In the cases of France and Spain, the *plans* include uniform financial statements for publication. In Belgium and West Germany, uniform financial statements are required instead by company law. An interesting irony is that West Germany is now the only country of the four not to have a compulsory accounting plan.

In many developing countries, particularly those influenced by France, accounting plans have also been introduced. It may well be that in the absence of large and listed companies, of many private shareholders and of a strong profession, the use of an accounting plan is more suitable than Anglo-Saxon judgemental accounting principles.

In Anglo-Saxon countries there has generally been much less uniformity. As far as formats for financial statements are concerned, there were no rules in law (before the 1981 UK Act and the 1983 Netherlands Act) and virtually no rules on formats in accounting standards. The requirements of the fourth Directive were based on German law and were revolutionary compared to previous Anglo-Dutch rules of this century. But even now there remains much more flexibility in the UK, Ireland and the Netherlands than in the rest of the EEC; and US flexibility of formats and terminology is greater still.

Turning to accounting principles, the control by company law, tax law or accounting plan has been substantial in most EEC countries. Though, again, in the UK, Ireland and the Netherlands (and in Australia and New Zealand), there have traditionally been no rules in company law apart from 'fairness'. The accountancy profession has been influential in inventing and policing the rules of valuation and measurement. In the UK and Ireland, Australia and New Zealand the Accounting Standards Committees have been controlled by the professional bodies. In the Netherlands, guidelines are published by the Council for Annual Reporting (*Raad voor Jaarrekening*) in which the Netherlands Institute of Registered Accountants plays the most influential role (see Nobes and Parker, 1985, Ch. 6). Particularly in Australia, the involvement of the government has recently increased (see Ch. 4; and Nobes and Parker, 1985, Ch. 3).

Standards and guidelines in these countries are not legally binding. In the UK and Ireland, non-compliance should lead to an audit qualification; in the Netherlands not even that. However, the legal requirement for 'fairness' would be likely to be interpreted by a Court with the aid of standards. In the Netherlands there is a special Enterprise Chamber of the Court of Justice especially for accounting cases (Klaassen, 1980). Nevertheless, there has been plenty of room for variety in Anglo-Saxon countries in the EEC and elsewhere. This is particularly true in the Netherlands, where replacement cost is used in statutory accounts by some companies, while others still use unsupplemented historical cost. However, the implementation of the fourth Directive has introduced many detailed rules into law for the first time. This has somewhat increased uniformity, but mainly it has raised problems between law and standards.

Further along the scale towards uniformity are the USA and Canada. In the USA, for companies within the scope of the SEC, the standards of the Financial Accounting Standards Board (FASB) are rather more powerful than UK accounting standards. The FASB is independent from (though influenced by) the accountancy profession, and has had partially delegated to it the function of setting standards by the federal government-controlled SEC. The SEC refuses to accept for filing the financial statements of companies which have not obeyed 'generally accepted accounting principles', which normally means statements of the FASB and predecessor bodies. In Canada, the professional accountancy body's standards are generally incorporated into law under the provisions of the Business Corporations Act of 1975. This has generally meant the adoption by 'regulation' of the profession's standards.

However, this rather stronger attitude to standard practice in North America does not imply anything like the uniformity to be found in France, because the standards still allow room for interpretation, flexibility and judgement (see Ch. 4 for an extended treatment of Anglo-Saxon rule making).

The remaining potential area of uniformity is disclosure requirements. One difference between Franco-German and Anglo-Saxon practice is that companies in the former countries tend to restrict their disclosures to legal requirements, except when seeking to raise Anglo-American finance. In the UK and the USA, the basic disclosures required by law are substantial and lead to considerable uniformity. However, other disclosures required by or recommended by the profession, or experimented with by individual companies, are common. This leads to a certain degree of variation.

3.8 Shareholder Orientation of Financial Statements

The first section of this chapter discussed the connection between 'fairness' and the predominance of outside shareholders. Shareholder orientation spreads further than accounting principles: it affects the format of financial statements. At its most obvious, the general use of a vertical format in the UK and the Netherlands rather than a horizontal format in West Germany or France suggests a greater shareholder orientation in the former countries. This is because the vertical format allows the presentation of working capital and net worth, and it contrasts net worth with shareholders' funds.

However, even in the horizontal version of the balance sheet (see Table 3.2), the UK version has greater shareholder orientation; it shows the shareholders' funds together, rather than showing the year's net profit as a separate item at the bottom of the balance sheet (or a loss at the bottom of the assets side!) as did the 1965 *Aktiengesetz*. The greater German interest in the double entry aspects of the balance sheet is demonstrated by the presentation of 'provisions for bad debts' as a liability , and 'called up share capital not paid' as the first asset. The new formats introduced in West Germany by the 1985 legislation to implement the fourth Directive remove many of these differences (Nobes, 1986; Brooks and Mertin, 1986).

Table 3.2 The Evolution of the Balance Sheet in the Fourth Directive (abbreviated versions)

	AktG (S 151)		*1971 Draft (Art. 8)*		*1981 Act (Format 2)*
Assets (shown on left)					
I	Unpaid capital	A	Unpaid capital	A	Unpaid capital
		B	Formation expenses		
II	Fixed and financial	C	Fixed assets	B	Fixed assets
	A Fixed and intangible		I Intangible		I Intangible
	B Financial		II Tangible		II Tangible
			III Participations		III Investments
III	Current Assets	D	Current assets	C	Current assets
	A Stocks		I Stocks		I Stocks
	B Other current		II Debtors		II Debtors
			III Securities		III Investments
					IV Cash
IV	Deferred charges	E	Prepayments	D	Prepayments
V	Accumulated losses	F	Loss		
			I For the year		
			II Brought forward		

Liabilities and capital (shown on right)

I	Share capital	A	Subscribed capital	A	Capital and reserves I Called up capital
II	Disclosed reserves	B	Reserves		II Share premium III Revaluation reserve IV Other reserves V Profit and loss
III	Provisions for diminutions	C	Value adjustments		
IV	Provisions for liabilities	D	Provisions for charges	B	Provisions for liabilities and charges
V	Liabilities (4 years +)	E	Creditors	C	Creditors
VI	Other liabilities				
VII	Deferred income	F	Accruals	D	Accruals
VIII	Profit	G	Profit I For the year II Brought forward		

The German-style profit and loss account (see Table 3.1 for 1965 Act example) is also probably less useful for decision-making than the normal Anglo-Saxon concentration on gross profit, net profit and 'earnings'. This is in addition to the problem of income smoothing discussed earlier. Further, disclosed calculations of earnings per share are normal only in the Anglo-Saxon world.

3.9 Conclusion

The eight areas of differences discussed above are amongst the more important variations in financial reporting practices, though they do not amount to a complete list. What is clear is that a reader would be seriously misled if he compared financial statements from apparently similar companies from various countries: the differences in asset valuation and profit measurement are very great.

References

Abel, R. (1969) 'A comparative simulation of German and US accounting principles', *Journal of Accounting Research*, Spring.

Beeny, J.H. (1975) *European Financial Reporting*, Vol. 1, ICAEW, London.

Brooks, J.P. and Mertin, D. (1986) *Neues deutsches Bilanzrecht: New German Accounting Legislation*, IDW Verlag, Düsseldorf.

Davidson, S. and Kohlmeier, J. (1966) 'A measure of the impact of some foreign accounting principles', *Journal of Accounting Research*, Autumn.

Donaghy, P.J. and Laidler, J. (1982) *European Financial Reporting*, Vol. 5, ICAEW, London.

Edwards, J.R. and Webb, K.M. (1984) 'The development of group accounting in the UK to 1933', *Accounting Historians Journal*, Spring.

Forester, D.A.R. (1977) *Schmalenbach and After*, Strathclyde Convergencies, Glasgow.

Gray, S.J. (1980) 'The impact of international accounting differences from a security-analysis perspective: some European evidence', *Journal of Accounting Research*, Spring.

Hein, L.W. (1978) *The British Companies Acts and the Practice of Accountancy 1844–1962*, Arno Press.

Klaassen, J. (1980) 'An accounting court: the impact of the Enterprise Chamber on financial reporting in the Netherlands', *Accounting Review*, April.

Minnis, E.P. and Nobes, C.W. (1985) *Accountants' Liability in the 1980s*, Croom Helm.

Most, K.S. (1971) 'The French accounting experiment', *International Journal of Accounting*, Fall.

Nobes, C.W. (1986) 'New laws for old: Germany leaps ahead', *Accountancy*, December.

Nobes, C.W. and Parker, R.H. (1985) *Comparative International Accounting*, 2nd edn, Philip Allan.

Payne, P.L. (1967) 'The emergence of the large-scale company in Great Britain, 1870–1914', *Economic History Review*, pp. 519–542.

Semler, J. (1962) 'The German accountant's approach to safeguarding investors' and creditors' interests', Paper at the Eighth International Congress of Accountants, reprinted in *The Australian Accountant*, September.

Singer, H.W. (1943) *Standardized Accountancy in Germany*, Cambridge University Press.

Walker, R.G. (1978) *Consolidated Statements*, Arno Press.

Further Reading

Choi, F.D.S. and Mueller, G.G. (1984) *International Accounting*, Chapters 3, 6 and 8, Prentice-Hall.

4

Regulating Financial Reporting in the UK, USA, Australia and Canada

ROBERT H. PARKER

4.1 Introduction

The similarities of company financial reporting in the major Anglo-Saxon countries (the USA, the UK, Canada and Australia) are well known and, indeed, the differences between them and continental European countries have been emphasised in previous chapters of this book.

A number of writers have eloquently illustrated these similarities. Carsberg (Nobes and Parker, 1985, p. 14), for example, has pointed out that the reader who expects to find dramatic differences between British and US accounting is likely to be disappointed:

> If an accountant crosses the Atlantic, he may experience an initial sense of shock at the discovery that the balance sheet appears to be presented upside down and that the financial statements are written in what seems to be a partially foreign language. However, after he has learned the language, he is likely to conclude that the similarities between British and American accounting greatly outweigh the differences. He will not find that he has to master an alien accounting philosophy.

A Canadian writer has seriously suggested that Canadians (and by implication the British and Australians as well) should accept the American Financial Accounting Standards Board (FASB) as the leading agency of accounting research in the English-speaking world:

> It is considering the same issues as we are, and it has far greater resources. Instead of going through the same motions as the FASB, we should accept its

> research and consider only whether there is anything in the Canadian context that would alter FASB conclusions for application in this country. We might also look for a way to participate directly with them, both intellectually and financially. (Sands, 1980, p. 6)

The chairman of the Australian National Companies and Securities Commission has asked: 'Would [Australia] be much worse off if we took the American or perhaps the Canadian standards and enforced them here . . .?' (Bosch, 1985).

These comments are not too surprising. All four countries are not only (in the main) English-speaking but they also share a similar legal system and business environment and are linked by many economic ties, including those of trade and investment. In all of them the accountancy profession is highly developed and institutionalised. Indeed, the five largest professional accountancy bodies in the world are, in order of size, the American Institute of Certified Public Accountants (AICPA), the (US) National Association of Accountants, the Institute of Chartered Accountants in England and Wales (ICAEW), the Australian Society of Accountants and the Canadian Institute of Chartered Accountants (CICA). These countries provided four out of the nine founding members of the International Accounting Standards Committee. The world's leading accountancy firms are overwhelmingly British and American in origin (Nobes and Parker, 1985, p. 6). In all four countries the organised accountancy profession has deliberately and voluntarily, to a much greater extent than in Continental Europe or Japan, involved itself in the regulation of accounting practice.

The present chapter will not dwell further on these similarities but will, instead, emphasise the differences. These appear not so much in the practice of financial reporting as in the way in which it is *regulated*. The type of regulation appears to be a function not of economic and commercial factors but of political, social, cultural and historical ones. Stamp (1980), for example, in making a comparison of the USA and Canada, and admitting the close similarities of financial accounting practice, was at pains to emphasise that: the history of the two countries is quite different; Canada's parliamentary system is based on the British not the US model; Canadians tend to adopt a less adversarial approach towards the solution of their problems; there is a greater emphasis on social justice and social welfare; wider corporate responsibility is more acceptable; and there is more public participation in the economy. He concluded that Canadians ought to continue to set their own accounting standards. Parker (1982) came to the same conclusion in relation to Australia.

It is certainly true that the ways in which accounting disclosure and measurement rules are set in the four countries differ quite considerably. Some examples of the nature of such rules are listed below in order to show, in a preliminary way, the diversity which currently exists.

(i) UK Statements of Standard Accounting Practice (SSAPs)
These are designed by an Accounting Standards Committee and approved by six professional accountancy bodies which 'enforce' them on companies only by persuasion and through control of auditors.

(ii) US Statements of Financial Accounting Standards (SFAS)
These are designed by the Financial Accounting Standards Board (FASB). Approval and enforcement, for SEC-registered companies, is given by a government regulatory body, the Securities and Exchange Commission (SEC).

(iii) Approved Accounting Standards of the Australian Accounting Standards Review Board (ASRB)
These are designed mainly by the Accounting Standards Board of the Australian Accounting Research Foundation (AARF) and approved first by that Committee's parents: the Institute of Chartered Accountants in Australia and the Australian Society of Accountants. Subsequently, and sometimes with amendments, they are approved by the ASRB. They are enforced by a requirement in the Companies Act and Codes to prepare financial statements 'in accordance with applicable approved accounting standards'.

(iv) Accounting and Auditing Recommendations contained in the CICA Handbook
The Canada Business Corporations Act 1975 and similar legislation in the major Canadian provinces indicates that accounting and disclosure requirements, as well as auditors' reports, shall, unless otherwise specified, be in accordance with the Recommendations. These have also been adopted as mandatory by the provincial Securities Commissions.

(v) Schedules to Companies Acts
Such schedules are included in the British Companies Act 1985, and the Australian Companies Act and Codes. The provisions have a legal authority which can be enforced in the courts.

(vi) Financial Reporting Releases of the US Securities and Exchange Commission
These (and earlier Accounting Series Releases) are issued by the SEC which can enforce its authority by administrative action.

4.2 Theoretical Framework

It is essential to put such diversity into some sort of theoretical framework. The one used in this chapter was developed by Puxty, Willmott, Cooper and Lowe (1987), who based it on the work of Streeck and Schmitter (1985).

There are several ways in which company financial reporting can be regulated. Three limiting and ideal cases are: through the 'market', the 'state' and the 'community'. If the process is left entirely to market forces each company chooses its own rules, influenced only by pressures from, in particular, the capital market. To some extent this was the position in the 'unregulated economies' of 19th-century Britain and New South Wales, and in the United States before the establishment of the SEC, where some companies voluntarily published accounting information and subjected themselves to audit (Watts and Zimmerman, 1983; Morris, 1984). At another extreme the whole process can be in the hands of the 'state', an organ of which decrees which practices are to be followed and provides an enforcement mechanism. As we shall see later, this can be accomplished in a number of different ways. The third ideal case is the emergence of rules through the 'spontaneous solidarity' of the community.

Within these three extremes, Puxty *et al.* (1987) usefully distinguish what they and others term 'liberalism', 'associationism', 'corporatism' and 'legalism'. (The barbarous English of this terminology is unfortunate, but little can be done about it.) As Figure 4.1 shows, in accounting regulation, market and state have predominated over community. The four modes of Puxty *et al.* form a continuum. At one extreme is liberalism, whereby regulation is provided exclusively by the discipline of market principles,

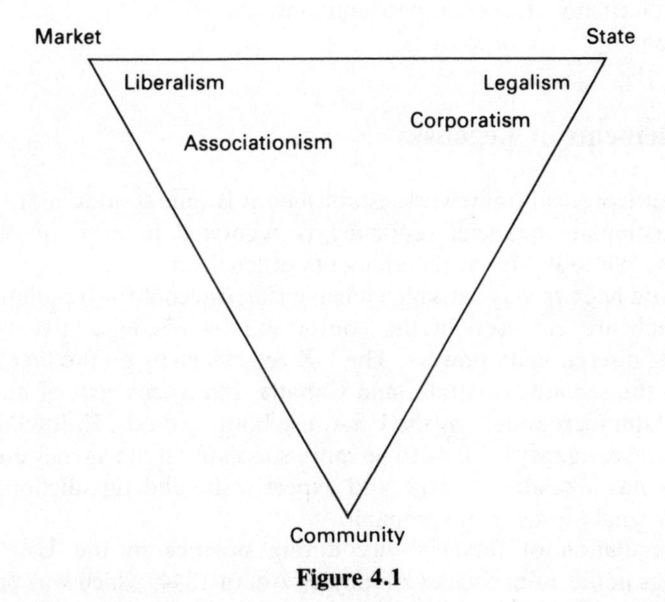

Figure 4.1

Source: Puxty et al. (1987), p. 283.

while companies provide information only if it is demanded commercially. At the other is legalism, which relies upon the unreserved application of state principles. Accounting practice is expected to follow the letter of the law, which is enforced by the state's monopoly of the means of coercion.

Within these two extremes are associationism and corporatism, both of which combine liberalism and legalism with a small dose of community influence. In associationism, regulation is accomplished through the development of organisations that are formed to represent and advance the interests of their members. These members form, of course, part of the community, but do not represent it as a whole. Corporatism involves a greater reliance upon the state principle of hierarchical control. The state does not simply license the existence of organised interest groups but incorporates them into its own centralised, hierarchical system of regulation. The basic difference between corporatism and associationism is the extent to which the state 'leans' on interest groupings to achieve public (i.e. state) as contrasted with private (i.e. market) purposes.

Puxty *et al*. apply this framework to the USA, the UK, West Germany and Sweden. Their conclusions are set out below. They did not apply their analysis to Australia or Canada.

USA	Elements of legalism and associationism, with the latter subordinated to the former.
UK	Principally associationist.
West Germany	Legalism predominant.
Sweden	Corporatist.

4.3 Elements of Legalism

With the theoretical framework established it is time to look more closely at how company financial reporting is regulated in each of our four countries. We look first at the elements of legalism.

The state has two ways in which it can enforce accounting regulations: by laws which are enforced in the courts and by administrative agencies exercising discretionary powers. The UK relies heavily on the first and the USA on the second. Australia and Canada, influenced first of all by the UK and later increasingly by the USA, use both methods. Enforcement by administrative agency is likely to be more successful if the agency enforcing the rules has a relatively large and expert staff, and jurisdiction over a relatively small number of companies.

The regulation of financial accounting practice in the UK has its beginnings in the Joint Stock Companies Act of 1844, which was based on the report of a Select Committee chaired by W.E. Gladstone. The device of a company law amendment committee to advise on desirable changes in the law was used on numerous occasions up to the 1960s. Throughout the nineteenth century, however, there were no mandatory accounting and audit regulations in the general Companies Acts, although railways, banks and public utilities were subject to much greater regulation. During the twentieth century the rules in the Acts have greatly increased in quantity and complexity. A notable landmark was the Companies Act 1947 (consolidated as the 1948 Act) which made group accounts compulsory, distinguished between 'reserves' and 'provisions' (thus making the creation of secret reserves more difficult), introduced many new disclosure requirements, and required directors to prepare (and auditors to report on) financial statements which were 'true and fair'. The Act was based on the 1945 Report of the Cohen Committee. The accounting and audit contents of both the Report and the Act were strongly influenced by the ICAEW.

The 1948 Act remained the principal act for almost 40 years but was amended by a series of Acts; the first in 1967 (which made the disclosure of turnover mandatory, greatly expanded the information to be provided in the Directors' Report and Notes, and removed the privilege of non-disclosure for family-owned private companies); another in 1976 (which tightened the legal requirements for the maintenance and publication of information, strengthened the power of auditors, and increased the disclosure of directors' interests); one in 1980 (which implemented the EEC second Directive); and one in 1981 (which implemented the EEC fourth Directive). In 1985 all these acts were consolidated into the Companies Act 1985, a 'jumbo' act of 747 sections and 25 schedules. Accounts and audit are dealt with more particularly in Parts VII, VIII, and XI(v) (Sections 221–281 and 384–394) and Schedules 4 to 11 of the Act.

Before 1981, company law contained mainly disclosure rules. These have been greatly expanded and many measurement rules have been added. Much is still left, however, to the Statements of Standard Accounting Practice issued by the accountancy profession. There is no *legal* requirement, for example, for UK companies to publish source and application of funds statements or to disclose earnings per share. Unlike legislators in the USA, Australia and Canada, British legislators have never seen the need to set up a securities commission with a strong interest in the regulation of corporate financial reporting. The main reason for this may lie in the close-knit nature of the City of London compared with the more scattered stock markets of the other countries. Also, of course, the British stock market crash in 1929 was by no means as severe as the American one.

The requirements of the UK Act, unlike those of the American SEC, apply to all British limited companies, large and small, except those few incorporated by royal charter or special act of parliament. The privatisation policy of the UK government in recent years has brought a number of very large public utilities within the net of company law. The basic requirements of the 1985 Act (Sections 227–228) are that all companies shall prepare a balance sheet and a profit and loss account which comply with the detailed requirements of the fourth Schedule, and give a true and fair view. The latter is nowhere defined but overrides the requirements of Schedule 4 and all other requirements of the Act 'as to the matters to be included in a company's accounts or in notes to those accounts'. If necessary, additional information must be provided and, in special circumstances, the detailed provisions must be departed from.

The fourth Schedule sets out both disclosure rules and measurement rules in some detail. The disclosure rules include mandatory formats for the balance sheet and profit and loss account, and lists of items to be disclosed in the Notes to the Accounts. The formats are derived from the EEC fourth Directive but the British government, unlike those in some other member states (e.g. West Germany and France) has deliberately left them as flexible as possible. Thus UK companies may choose between two balance sheet formats and four profit and loss account formats. The published financial statements of UK companies (especially profit and loss accounts, and again unlike those of their German and French counterparts) do not at first sight greatly resemble the formats in the legislation. This is mainly because, apart from main headings, much detail is allowed to be shown in the Notes and partly because the formats are sometimes followed in spirit rather than to the letter.

The measurement rules, although introduced as a result of the EEC fourth Directive, are consistent with previously generally accepted UK practice. The accounting principles laid down (going concern, consistency, prudence, accruals and separate valuation) are largely those of SSAP 2. The 'historical cost accounting rules' set out in the fourth Schedule differ only slightly (e.g. by expressly allowing the use of LIFO) from those of UK SSAPs, and the alternative accounting rules are wide enough to allow the modification of historical cost by the revaluation of tangible fixed assets (a common UK practice) or current cost accounting (CCA). Where the historical cost accounting rules are departed from, additional information must be provided.

By the time that the regulation of company financial reporting became an issue, the USA had, unlike Australia and Canada, long lost its colonial status. Also, unlike the UK, it had developed a federal political system. The legal framework of company financial reporting in the USA has developed along quite different lines to that in the UK. Although each state has its own Corporations Act, these have never included any accounting regulations of consequence and, until the early 1930s, financial reporting of companies in general (as distinct from that of railways and public utilities) was almost completely unregulated. Before the passing of the Securities Act 1933 and the Securities Exchange Act 1934 'liberalism' was predominant. The second of these Acts set up the Securities and Exchange Commission (SEC), a federal government agency with authority to determine the accounting and auditing practices required under the Acts. A significant difference from the UK position is that only about 11,000 corporations in the late 1980s (generally the largest) are subject to the jurisdiction of the SEC.

The establishment of the SEC led to 'associationism' as well as 'legalism' since one of the Commission's most important early decisions (expressed in Accounting Series Release No. 4, 25 April 1938) was to limit itself to a largely supervisory role. Financial statements 'prepared in accordance with accounting principles for which there is no substantial authoritative support' were presumed to be misleading or inaccurate even if accompanied by extra disclosure. The SEC has found its source of authority in, successively, the Committee on Accounting Procedure of the American Institute of Accountants (now the AICPA), the Accounting Principles Board (APB) of the AICPA, and the Financial Accounting Standards Board (FASB). Its recognition of the FASB is stated in ASR No. 150 (1973), where it is reaffirmed that 'without abdicating its responsibilities the Commission has historically looked to the standard-setting bodies designated by the profession to provide leadership in establishing and improving accounting principles'.

The SEC's approach, which has not been without its vigorous critics (e.g. Chatov, 1975; Kripke, 1979), has meant that US generally accepted accounting principles (GAAP) are to be found *not* in legislation, nor even in ASRs (now FRRs), *but* mainly in the Statements of Financial Accounting Standards (SFASs) of the FASB and, to the extent that they have not been superseded, in the Accounting Research Bulletins (ARBs) of the Committee on Accounting Procedure, and in the Opinions of the APB.

The SEC has, however, been careful to maintain its supervisory role and Congress itself has not hesitated to intervene on occasion (Nobes and Parker, 1985, pp. 16–19). The SEC has intervened on inflation accounting and on oil and gas accounting, and Congress on the accounting treatment of the investment tax credit. Committees of Congress have criticised the role of the FASB in setting accounting standards. The highly detailed nature of US GAAP, the ultimate governmental sanctions behind it, and the intervention of the SEC and Congress in crucial areas, justify the appellation of 'legalism' to the way in which SEC-registered companies are regulated. On the other hand the considerable input and influence of the accountancy profession demonstrates a strong element of 'associationism'.

Unlike the USA, in Australia financial reporting remained strongly influenced by the UK until the 1960s. Australians copied without hesitation the British system of incorporating financial reporting rules into companies legislation. However, given a federal political framework, this meant not one Companies Act but several. Each of the states had a Companies Act which contained a fairly detailed set of disclosure rules but almost no measurement rules. Until the 1960s these Acts tended to be lagged versions of British legislation, although the State of Victoria was notably innovative. The inconvenience of different requirements was recognised in the early 1960s when the Acts, by agreement among the states, became more or less uniform. In the 1970s, however, the Acts started to diverge again, and this, plus the perceived need to regulate the stock markets more closely, led in 1978 to a formal agreement between the federal government and the states, the purpose of which was to achieve uniformity in company law and its administration.

Two central bodies were set up: a Ministerial Council for Companies and Securities and a National Companies and Securities Commission (NCSC). The Ministerial Council, comprising the Attorneys General of the states and the commonwealth, is a policy-making body which recommends to the commonwealth (i.e. federal) and state governments any changes which require legislation. Administration of the legislation is delegated to the NCSC, which in turn delegates the day-to-day administration to the Commissioners for Corporate Affairs of each state. The NCSC, although obviously modelled on the SEC, differs in important respects. It is responsible for *all* companies, not just the largest, but at the same time it lacks the considerable financial and staff resources of its American counterpart. It is more difficult politically in Australia than in the USA to entrust important regulatory powers to a federal body.

Uniformity of company legislation has been achieved in a manner which preserves the rights of the states. The Commonwealth Government enacted in 1981 a Companies Act which applies only in the Australian Capital Territory (ACT). Each state has adopted this Act as a 'Companies Code'. The accounting requirements of the Companies Act and Codes are detailed and important. Much of the detail is in the Companies Regulations made under the Act. The basic requirements (s. 269) are that all companies shall prepare a balance sheet and a profit and loss account which give a true and fair view and, without affecting the generality of this provision, comply with the detailed requirements of the seventh Schedule to the Companies Regulations. Australia did not amend the true and fair requirement in the way that the UK did in 1981.

The seventh Schedule (as amended in 1986) prescribes formats for financial statements and differential disclosure for different types of companies (Walton, 1987). The formats cover the profit and loss account (starting with operating profit or loss) and the balance sheet. The language used draws on both American and British terminology. The formats are those suitable for consolidated accounts. The remainder of the Schedule is mainly concerned with disclosure rules, although, for example, it is expressly required that intercompany transactions and balances shall be eliminated in the preparation of consolidated accounts. There is no mention of historical cost accounting rules or alternative accounting rules. Companies are classified for disclosure purposes as exempt proprietary (defined in terms of shareholding), non-exempt, and large non-exempt (with size measured in terms of total assets and sales). Each class must disclose specified information in the Notes. There are also special disclosure requirements for borrowing and guarantor corporations and for listed companies.

A major difference from the UK position is that Australian companies must, subject to giving a true and fair view, prepare accounts in accordance with 'applicable approved accounting standards'. These are accounting standards as approved by the Accounting Standards Review Board (ASRB), established not by legislation but by Ministerial Council. The relationship between approved accounting standards and the Australian accounting standards (AASs) issued by the accountancy profession is explained in the next section of this chapter.

Canada was at first strongly influenced by UK developments in financial reporting but later the USA took over as the major external influence. Like the USA and Australia, Canada is a federation. The looseness of the Canadian federation has produced only provincial securities commissions but there is federal as well as provincial company legislation. The companies acts had little effect on disclosure by commercial and industrial corporations until the 1907 Ontario Companies Act, on which later federal requirements for financial statement disclosure were based. The 1953 Ontario Companies Act was equally influential. Both in turn were strongly influenced by the recommendations of the Institute of Chartered Accountants of Ontario (ICAO). Members of ICAO and of the other provincial institutes are also members of the Canadian Institute of Chartered Accountants (CICA) which since 1968 has promulgated its accounting recommendations in a *CICA Handbook*. The recommendations were given official recognition in the 1970s by the securities commissions and by the federal and provincial legislatures. Recognition came first in the Canadian Securities Administrators National Policy Statement No. 27 (1972) (a document without the force of law). This was followed a few years later by the (federal) Canada Business Corporations Act 1975, which transferred the requirements relating to financial statements from the body of the Act to a more easily altered Regulations Section and required the statements to conform to generally accepted accounting principles as set out in the *CICA Handbook*. The Ontario Securities Act 1978 and other provincial legislation contain the same requirement.

The influence of American practice is shown by the Ontario Securities Act 1966, which designated the Ontario Securities Commission (OSC) as the body to oversee the Toronto Stock Exchange and gave the OSC powers not unlike those of the SEC. The OSC has, however, never countermanded a standard set by the CICA. This degree of delegation to the profession of the making of enforceable rules is unique to Canada. Murphy (1986, p. 32) explains it as due to 'the early organisation and leadership of the Institute of Chartered Accountants of Ontario (ICAO), the vigour and interest of the Office of the Provincial Secretary of Ontario, the untarnished prominence and strength of the CICA and Canadian good fortune in having few corporate scandals – relative to the United States and Britain – that rebounded to any enduring discredit of the accounting profession.'

4.4 Associationism or Corporatism?

As already noted, both associationism and corporatism combine liberalism and legalism with a small dose of community influence. The difference is that organised interest groups such as the accountancy profession are more integrated into the mechanism of the state under corporatism than under associationism.

In all four countries, setting accounting standards has become a major activity of the accountancy profession. Conceptually, three phases of standard setting can be distinguished (Morley, 1985):

(i) a **design** phase in which a particular aspect of accounting is identified and researched and an exposure draft is prepared;
(ii) an **approval** phase in which the draft is subjected to review and, if it survives, approved as a standard;
(iii) an **enforcement** phase in which compliance is monitored and, if necessary, appropriate remedial action is taken.

Professional accountancy bodies are, it can be argued, the most suitable group to be entrusted with the design phase. In Anglo-Saxon countries, not only are they likely to have the most competence technically but they may be the only group willing to undertake the task. Accountancy bodies in these countries are usually strongly influenced by, if not under the control of, firms of public accountants, but may also include accountants in industry and commerce who are suppliers of financial information and are often part of company management.

Accountancy bodies are much less well equipped to handle the final, enforcement phase, since they have no power to enforce compliance with their standards by non-members (e.g. directors of companies). On the basis of American evidence, Moonitz (1974) concluded that a private accountancy body is unlikely to obtain such power and that company management would not willingly stand by to let the profession set the standards by which reported financial position and the results of operations are determined. His recommendation is that the profession should become the technical advisor to the agency that possesses the power to enforce the rules. Such a role seems to imply corporatism rather than associationism. The intermediate (approval) phase requires both technical and political skills and is not always easily distinguishable from the other phases.

The description of regulation in the UK as principally associationist (Puxty *et al.*, 1987) is justified by the UK profession's relative independence from state control in its standard setting and by its influence on legislation. Professional accountants were influential members of the various company law amendment committees. The evidence given by the professional accountancy bodies to the Greene and Cohen Committees helped to shape the very different approaches to financial reporting of the 1929 and 1948 Companies Acts. The latter was particularly influenced by the Recommendations on Accounting Principles issued by the Institute of Chartered Accountants in England and Wales from 1942 onwards. The requirement that companies give a 'true and fair view' was first suggested by representatives of the ICAEW.

When company financial reporting was subjected to increasing public criticism in the late 1960s, the ICAEW responded by forming an Accounting Standards Steering Committee (later renamed Accounting Standards Committee, ASC, and joined by the other professional accountancy bodies). Membership of the ASC has varied but the Committee has always been relatively large, with unpaid part-time members, drawn largely, although by no means entirely, from the profession. It issues exposure drafts (EDs) for comment by interested parties. Most EDs are later issued in amended form (by each of the six professional accountancy bodies, not by the ASC itself) as Statements of Standard Accounting Practice (SSAPs). SSAPs contain both disclosure rules (e.g. SSAP 10 on funds statements) and measurement rules (e.g. SSAP 4 on government grants). Some SSAPs are a mixture of both sets of rules; e.g. SSAP 3 which requires both the disclosure of earnings per share (not required by the Companies Act) and the rules by which it is to be calculated. Most SSAPs apply to all companies (SSAP 3, which applies only to listed companies, is one of the few exceptions) and indeed to all entities which are required by law, or choose voluntarily, to present accounts that give a true and fair view.

Although SSAPs have merely persuasive authority, since the UK professional accountancy bodies have disciplinary powers over their own members only, much of the profession's rule-making has been accepted by government, commerce and industry. Indeed, just as some of the Recommendations of the English Institute were incorporated into the Companies Act 1948 so have some parts of SSAPs been incorporated into the Companies Act 1985 (via the Fourth Directive).

On the other hand, in some critical areas, in particular inflation accounting, the ASC has notably failed to produce acceptable rules.

Recent SSAPs on goodwill and business combinations have been heavily criticised for their permissiveness. The recent introduction of Statements of Recommended Practice (SORPs), akin to the old Recommendations, means that some industries, e.g. oil and gas, are being allowed and encouraged to prepare their own accounting rules for 'franking' or approval. The ASC has made little attempt to construct a conceptual framework.

A number of committees have looked at the standard-setting process in the UK. The most recent was set up by the Consultative Committee of Accountancy Bodies (CCAB) in 1987. The committee is under the chairmanship of Sir Ronald Dearing, a non-accountant. The committee will consider, *inter alia*, the most appropriate form that accounting standards should take; the status of standards in relation to company law; procedures for the monitoring of compliance with standards and the enforcement of standards; the identification of topics for consideration; the need for, and nature of, public consultation about draft standards; the funding of the cost of standard setting; and the membership and powers of the standard-setting body.

The American FASB differs from the British ASC in many important respects. Unlike its predecessor, the APB, it is not under direct control of the AICPA, although some of its members have been practising CPAs at the time of appointment. There are only seven members, all of whom are full-time and well paid, severing their connections with their previous employers. They are appointed by the Financial Accounting Foundation and advised by the Financial Accounting Standards Advisory Council. In developing standards the FASB follows a complex 'due process' procedure that for major projects includes task forces, discussion memoranda, public hearings and exposure drafts. Due process can be very time-consuming. For this reason the FASB established, in 1984, an Emerging Issues Task Force (EITF) which meets about every six weeks and whose objective is to seek to determine whether the existing accounting literature can support a consensus for treating new accounting problems without the necessity for the Board to issue a formal pronouncement.

As well as SFASs, the Board issues Statements of Financial Accounting Concepts (SFACs), Interpretations and Technical Bulletins. The SFACs are the output of the FASB's conceptual framework project and do not form part of GAAP. Such a framework may be more relevant to private sector bodies whose standards will be enforced, if approved, by a public sector agency, than to bodies whose standards are not enforced in this manner. Perhaps this is a measure of the relative predominance of legalism and associationism. All this considerable activity is backed up by financial and staffing resources well in excess of those enjoyed by any private sector standard-setting body in any other country.

The backing of the SEC ensures full compliance with SFASs by US companies subject to its jurisdiction. Such complete compliance is not achieved in the UK. Also, whereas a British accountant is constantly referring to the Companies Act as well as SSAPs, an American accountant is mainly concerned to follow the rules of the FASB and its predecessors. In practice, however, on critical issues, this may not mean that the FASB is much more powerful than the ASC. Inflation accounting provides an example. The attempt by the FASB to issue a standard favouring general price level accounting was frustrated by the SEC, as was the ASC's similar attempt to introduce current purchasing power accounting by the establishment of a government committee. Both eventually produced standards which leaned entirely (SSAP 16) or partially (SFAS 33) towards replacement cost accounting. SFAS 33 achieved in the short term greater compliance and lasted longer, but both have now effectively been withdrawn.

Neither Australia nor Canada have closely followed the UK or US precedents. In Australia developments were at first very similar to those in the UK, with Australian accounting standards (AASs) designed by the Accounting Standards Board of the Australian Accounting Research Foundation (AARF) and issued, after approval, by each of the two major professional bodies, the Institute of Chartered Accountants in Australia (ICAA) and the Australian Society of Accountants (ASA). AASs have much the same authority as UK SSAPs. The professional bodies preferred the Canadian solution of giving legal backing to the profession's standards rather than the establishment of an Accounting Standards Review Board (ASRB). In terms of Murphy's (1986) explanation of the circumstances in which such backing can be achieved, it may be hazarded that the leadership of the profession was too disputed (amalgamation of the ICAA and ASA, although attempted, has never succeeded and there is no equivalent of the CICA); that there was no political support (the Attorneys General have tended to criticise rather than support the efforts of the profession); and that Australia has not been lacking in corporate scandals for which the accountancy profession has been allotted, fairly or not, some of the blame.

Once the ASRB had been established, the profession naturally hoped that its own standards would be recognised as 'applicable approved accounting standards' and it has in any case continued to issue them on the grounds that AASs are intended for use by a wider range of enterprises than those covered by the Companies Act and Codes.

The ASRB has faced many problems, and opinions differ about the extent to which it has been 'captured' by the accountancy profession (Walker, 1987; Parker, Peirson and Ramsay, 1987). The profession has certainly been very influential. Members of the Board (seven in number – as for the FASB) are part-time and appointed by the Ministerial Council from panels of names submitted by a number of interested organisations (including ICAA, ASA and AARF). They need not all be accountants but in practice all have been. Standards may be submitted by anybody, not just the profession, but in practice the Board has concerned itself very largely with AASs. There has been a battle of priorities: the ASRB has not hesitated to let the AARF know what standards it would like to have submitted and, in its turn, the AARF has not always readily accepted the ASRB's suggestions and has attempted to maintain its own priorities.

The ASRB has regarded its function as being one of amendment as well as approval and has also attempted to redraft the profession's standards to make them more legally precise. At the same time the Board's perceived slowness to approve standards in its early years has resulted, through pressure from the NCSC, in the adoption of 'fast track' procedures which have led the ASRB merely to advertise that it is considering releasing a standard in a form similar to that of the relevant AAS, rather than redrafting it before public exposure. Like the FASB, the ASRB has felt the need for some sort of conceptual framework. Lacking the former's resources, it has produced so far a list of ten 'assumptions'. At the same time the AARF has been working on its own conceptual framework.

The rules of Australian financial reporting are now to be found in the Companies Act and Codes and in two sets of accounting standards, only one set of which is mandatory. The status of AARF standards which have either not been submitted for approval or are still in the process of being approved is unclear. The status of those AARF standards which diverge from equivalent ASRB standards is also unclear. Some critics have argued that the ASRB is unnecessary because it merely duplicates the work done by the profession. What is the point, it is argued, of letting one set of accountants criticise, at public expense, the work of another set of accountants? There have been calls for a merger of the AARF and the ASRB. At the time of writing it is unclear whether such a merger will take place and, if it does, how this will affect the profession's influence over standard setting. The Ministerial Council has agreed that much of the disclosure requirements in the seventh Schedule should be progressively transferred to approved accounting standards. In conclusion, the regulation of Australian reporting is currently in a state of flux and it remains unclear whether the system is best described as corporatism or associationism.

In Canada the corporations and securities legislation of the federal government and the provinces requires companies to follow, to a large exent, the requirements of the *CICA Handbook* (Drummond and Mason, 1985, p. viii). These requirements are designed by the Accounting Standards Committee of the CICA. The Committee, which is divided into four geographic sections, normally comprises 21 part-time, unpaid members and includes accountants in public practice, commerce, finance and education as well as a minority of non-accountants. Not fewer than two thirds are members of the CICA. Up to six Committee members are appointed, after consultation with the Committee's Chairman and CICA's General Director of Research, by other organisations, such as the Canadian Council of Financial Analysts, the Financial Executives Institute of Canada and the Society of Management Accountants of Canada. The Committee is empowered to review matters of accounting theory and practice and, with the written approval of at least two-thirds of its voting members, to issue on its own authority such recommendations as it considers will be of benefit to the public, including users, preparers and auditors of financial information (*CICA Handbook*, Introduction to Accounting Recommendations, March 1985).

There is also an Accounting Research Advisory Board whose intended function is to provide a forum for discussion of the views of a cross-section of those who are affected by, and who have an important role in, the acceptance of Accounting Recommendations as set out in, or proposed for, the *CICA Handbook* and the studies that precede them. The Advisory Board formally participates in the process of setting priorities for the Committee on the initial or continued development of new Recommendations, the reconsideration of existing Recommendations and the undertaking of Accounting Research Studies. The board normally consists of ten to fifteen members, including lawyers and economists and senior representatives from finance, manufacturing, labour, the financial press, business and the universities.

Like the FASB, the CICA Accounting Standards Committee follows a complex due process procedure. It does not hold public hearings but, preceding the exposure draft stage, it circulates for comment to a limited group of people nominated by members of the Accounting Standards Committee a proposed 'Statement of Principles'.

Also included in the *CICA Handbook* are 'Guidelines' prepared by an Accounting Standards Steering Committee, acting under authority delegated by the Accounting Standards Committee. These Guidelines have been published when it was deemed that a pronouncement could not wait for the lengthy due process that precedes a Recommendation. It is assumed that a Guideline will eventually be replaced by a Recommendation. In recent years the number of Guidelines has grown and the securities commissions have tended to give them the same status as Recommendations.

Waterhouse (1982) investigated how this system works in practice. His findings suggested that Committee members did not perceive their activities as predominantly political or legislative. The then chairman of the Committee expressed surprise at this finding (Ward, 1982, p. 137). A possible explanation is that perceiving or admitting to a political function may decrease the legitimacy of the professional person acting as a standard setter, who may therefore attempt to define the problem of which standards should be adopted in technical, conceptual or professional terms

(Waterhouse, p. 147). Members' decisions were apparently based on practical experience rather than on conceptual considerations or on economic consequences. Waterhouse also reported that the Committee received little feedback on its proposals except from a relatively small number of large businesses and accounting firms. Most of the Committee's proposals appeared to enjoy broadly based support, especially those that were consistent with US accounting standards. By and large Canadian pronouncements on particular topics have in fact been modelled on US ones, and have rarely preceded them (Skinner, 1982, p. 164). On the other hand, Waterhouse's respondents were adamant that US standards should not prevail in Canada even for Canadian companies registered with the SEC in the USA, or for Canadian subsidiaries of US corporations. The dominance of CICA in the Canadian standard-setting process has not gone unchallenged by the other major professional accountancy body, the Canadian Certified General Accountants' Association (CCGAA) which has taken the initiative of setting up an 'Accounting Standards Authority of Canada' and has invited, without success, CICA and the Society of Management Accountants of Canada (SMAC) to join them. The Canadian approach to standard setting cannot be called legalistic and it would appear to be more associationist than corporatist.

4.5 Summary

This chapter has concentrated on the ways in which corporate financial reporting in the four major Anglo-Saxon countries is different rather than similar. The differences relate not so much to financial reporting practice as to the ways in which it is regulated. These appear to be the result of political rather than economic factors and are analysed in terms of the relative predominance of 'liberalism', 'legalism', 'corporatism' and 'associationism'.

There are elements of legalism in all four countries but it takes different forms. In the UK, company legislation has long been the prime mode of accounting regulation. The legislation has generally, however, owed much to the prior initiatives of the accountancy profession. In the USA financial reporting was almost unregulated until the establishment of the Securities and Exchange Commission in the 1930s. Throughout its existence the SEC has generally limited itself to a supervisory role, but it has not hesitated, on occasion, to intervene directly in the standard-setting process. Australia has in recent years added to the company legislation (inherited from Britain) a National Companies and Securities Commission modelled on the SEC and an innovatory Accounting Standards Review Board. Canada also inherited British company law but has added provincial (not federal) securities commissions and a throughgoing delegation of accounting rulemaking to the profession.

Professional rulemaking (whether or not regarded as such by the accountancy bodies concerned) is a notable feature of Anglo-Saxon, as compared to continental European, corporate financial reporting, but the strength of the profession varies from country to country. The regulation of accounting in the UK may be regarded as principally associationist, given the profession's relative independence from state control in its standard setting, and its influence on legislation. In the USA, regulation is both legalist and associationist, but the relative independence of the FASB from the profession and the ultimate authority of the SEC suggest a predominance of legalism. Australia has witnessed a struggle between a standard-setting body set up by the profession and one set up by the state. It is as yet unclear whether their merger would symbolise corporatism or associationism. In Canada the profession's hold on accounting standard setting is much firmer and the regulatory mode more associationist than corporatist.

References

Basu, S. and Milburn, J.A. (eds) (1982) *Research to Support Standard Setting in Financial Accounting: A Canadian Perspective*, The Clarkson Gordon Foundation, Toronto.

Bosch, H. (1985) 'Profit is a measure', Address to the Accounting Association of Australia and New Zealand, Sydney, 26 August.

Chatov, R. (1975) *Corporate Financial Reporting – Public or Private Control?*, The Free Press.

Drummond, C.S.R. and Mason, A.K. (1985) *Guide to Accounting Pronouncements and Sources*, Butterworth.

Kripke, H. (1979) *The SEC and Corporate Disclosure: Regulation in Search of a Purpose*, Harcourt Brace Jovanovich.

Moonitz, M. (1974) *Obtaining Agreement on Standards in the Accounting Profession*, Studies in Accounting Research No. 8, American Accounting Association.

Morley, B.A. (1985) 'The ASRB – its role and current issues', Paper presented at the Victoria State Congress of the Institute of Chartered Accountants in Australia, Hobart, 18 April.

Morris, R.D. (1984) 'Corporate disclosure in a substantially unregulated environment', *Abacus*, June.

Murphy, George J. (1986) 'A chronology of the development of corporate financial reporting in Canada', *Accounting Historians Journal*, Spring.

Nobes, C.W. and Parker, R.H. (1985) *Comparative International Accounting*, 2nd edn, Philip Allan.

Parker, R.H. (1982) 'Why are Australian accounting standards different?', *Australian Accountant*, August.

Parker, R.H., Peirson, G. and Ramsay, A.L. (1987) 'Australian accounting standards and the law', *Companies and Securities Law Journal*, November.

Puxty, A.G., Willmott, Hugh C., Cooper, David J. and Lowe, Tony (1987) 'Modes of regulation in advanced capitalism: locating accountancy in four countries', *Accounting, Organizations and Society*, Vol. 12, No. 3.
Sands, J.E. (1980) 'Millions wasted?', Letter to *CA Magazine*, November.
Skinner, R.M. (1982) 'Research and standard setting in financial accounting – an illustrative case', in S. Basu and J.A. Milburn (1982) *op. cit.*, pp. 153–202.
Stamp, E. (1980) 'Accounting standard setting: a new beginning – evolution, not revolution', *CA Magazine*, September.
Streeck, W. and Schmitter, P.C. (1985) 'Community, market, state – and associations', in their *Private Interest Government and Public Policy*, Sage.
Walker, R.G. (1987) 'Australia's ASRB: a case study of political activity and regulatory "capture"', *Accounting and Business Research*, Summer.
Walton, P. (1987) 'Disclosure in financial statements – the new Schedule 7', *Companies and Securities Law Journal*, November.
Ward, D.G. (1982) 'Discussants' comments', in S. Basu and J.A. Milburn (1982) *op. cit.*, pp. 135–139.
Waterhouse, J.H. (1982) 'A descriptive analysis of selected aspects of the Canadian accounting standard-setting process', in S. Basu and J.A. Milburn *op. cit.*, pp. 95–134.
Waterhouse, J.H. (1982) 'Reply to discussants' comments', in S. Basu and J.A. Milburn, *op. cit.*, pp. 146–149.
Watts, R. and Zimmerman, J. (1983) 'Agency problems, auditing, and the theory of the firm: some evidence', *Journal of Law and Economics*, October.

Addendum

In 1988, the Australian federal government announced that it intended to legislate for the replacement of the National Companies and Securities Commission by an Australian Securities Commission, responsible to the Federal Attorney General.

Part III
ACCOUNTING PROBLEMS OF PARTICULAR RELEVANCE TO MNEs

5

Consolidation after the Seventh Directive

ROBERT H. PARKER
CHRISTOPHER W. NOBES

5.1 Background

The diversity of consolidation accounting theory and practice throughout the world is well attested (Nobes and Parker, 1985, Ch. 10). Harmonisation has been attempted on a world-wide basis by the International Accounting Standards Committee through IAS 3 (1976) and IAS 22 (1983), and on a regional level by the EEC. The latter's contribution is the seventh Directive, adopted by the Council of Ministers in 1983 and due for implementation in the late 1980s. Some member states have already fully or partially implemented the Directive.

The purpose of the present chapter is briefly to outline the provisions of the Directive and then to discuss its present and potential impact on consolidation accounting both within and outside the European Community.

Consolidated financial statements were first used in the USA nearly a century ago but did not become popular in the UK until the 1930s (later still in continental Europe). They are first mentioned in legislation in the UK in 1947, in West Germany in 1965, and in France in 1985. In the late 1980s they are still uncommon in many member states of the EEC. Different techniques have been used in different countries although US and UK methods have always been reasonably close, not least because the UK has tended to follow US rules or practices. 'Anglo-Saxon' methods of consolidation have been encouraged by the IASC.

The EEC has been harmonising company law for over 20 years (Nobes and Parker, 1985, Ch. 13). The most important Directives for company accounting are the fourth, which deals with the formats and rules of non-consolidated accounting, and the seventh which extends the rules to consolidated accounts. The fourth Directive did not deal with consolidations, partly because of the EEC Commission's 'salami' approach to harmonisation, and partly because, when it was first discussed, the UK was not a member state and consolidations were comparatively rare on the continent. However, the UK, when implementing the fourth Directive in 1981, made some of its provisions apply to groups as well. West Germany implemented the fourth, seventh and eighth Directives all in one go in 1985. There are several references in the text of the seventh Directive to clauses of the fourth. Laws implementing the seventh Directive (itself adopted in 1983) were required to be enacted by 1988, and their provisions were to apply by 1990.

5.2 Main Features of the Seventh Directive

Table 5.1 lists the main provisions of the Directive and the major source country for each provision. The paragraphs which follow give further information on the provisions relating to: definition of a group, exemptions, exclusions, special cases, accounting rules, disclosure in the notes and directors' report, and audit. The problem areas of goodwill (difference on consolidation) and associated undertakings (equity method and proportional consolidation) are discussed at greater length in Section 5.5.

Table 5.1 Main Provisions of the Seventh Directive

Article		*Some source countries*
1	Subsidiaries are defined largely in terms of ownership, not control	UK, IRL, NL
3	Consolidation to include foreign subsidiaries	UK, IRL, NL, F
4	Consolidation irrespective of legal form of subsidiary	WG
4	Consolidation by all types of company	UK, IRL, NL
7	Exemption from preparation of group accounts by wholly-owned subsidiaries	UK, IRL, NL, F
16	True and fair view	UK, IRL, NL
17	Uniform formats to be used	WG, F
19	Goodwill to be calculated at date of first consolidation	UK, IRL, NL
19	Goodwill to be based on fair values	UK, IRL, NL
29	Tax-based valuations to be 'corrected' or at least disclosed	UK, IRL, NL
30	Goodwill to be depreciated or written off	UK, IRL, NL
33	Equity method for associated companies	UK, IRL, NL, F

Definition of a Group

The Directive compromises between the 'parent company concept' and the 'entity concept' with a leaning towards the former (Nobes and Parker, 1985, Ch. 10). Consolidation is required in all the following circumstances (Art. 1), i.e. when there is:

(a) a majority of the share voting rights;
(b) a shareholding plus a right to appoint or remove a majority of the directors;
(c) a dominant influence pursuant to a control contract (shareholding not necessary);
(d) a shareholding plus a majority of the voting rights.

Also, member states *may* require consolidation where there is:

(e) a participating interest plus an actual dominant influence or unified management.

Exemptions

There is no exemption for foreign subsidiaries (Art. 3), but member states may grant exemption where the parent is not a limited company (Art. 4). Subject to certain conditions, parents not listed on a stock exchange and which are themselves wholly-owned subsidiaries of a member state company are exempt from drawing up consolidated accounts (Art. 7). This exemption is extended to 90%-owned subsidiaries where the remaining 10 per cent approve the exemption. Member states may further extend exemption to other subsidiaries, and to subsidiaries of non-member state companies if the consolidated accounts are drawn up in accordance with the seventh Directive or 'in a manner equivalent'.

This final exemption proved controversial during the drafting of the Directive. An obvious problem is how to define and verify 'equivalence'. During negotiations for the Directive it was variously suggested that equivalence should be verified by an EEC auditor or that bilateral agreements should be made between the EEC and other countries to define which non-EEC consolidations could be accepted. Both these suggestions were eventually rejected. Further controversy has attended implementation. For example, the draft Dutch legislation referred to an earlier Ministry of Justice ruling which refers to IAS 3 for equivalence. This was not acceptable to the Commission.

Exemptions *may* be granted to:

(a) financial holding companies (Art. 5);
(b) small groups (as measured by turnover, balance sheet total, and number of employees; see Table 5.2 for the West German example) except where any member of the group is a listed company (Art. 6).

Both these exemptions were necessary in order to achieve adoption of the Directive. Financial holding companies are important in Luxembourg and some member states still lack the accounting resources for universal consolidation to be a practical possibility.

Exclusions

Subsidiaries may be excluded from consolidation (Arts. 13 and 14) on the grounds of:

(a) materiality;
(b) severe long-term restrictions;
(c) information unobtainable without disproportionate expense or undue delay;
(d) shares held exclusively with a view to subsequent resale;
(e) different activities (exclusion is obligatory if it is necessary to enable a true and fair view).

Table 5.2 West German Size Criteria

	Balance sheet total (DM mn)	*Sales (DM mn)*	*Number of employees*
OLD (Publicity Law, 1969):			
Consolidated statements	> 125	> 250	> 5,000
NEW (Accounting Directives Law, Art. 293):			
Consolidated statements	> 39.0	> 80	> 500
Combined statements*	> 46.8	> 96	> 500

Note: *Simple aggregation of parent and subsidiary figures.

Special Cases

Two articles in the Directive deal, though not explicitly, with the particular problems of the Anglo-Dutch multinationals, Unilever and Shell. The present practices of these companies are explained in Figure 5.1 which contains extracts from their 1987 Annual Reports. Unilever PLC and Unilever NV are not linked vertically but are managed on a unified basis. Article 12 allows member states to require a 'horizontal consolidation' in such a case. Shell Transport and Trading p.l.c and its linked company, Royal Dutch Petroleum, are parent companies that do not carry on any industrial or commercial activity but hold shares in subsidiary undertakings on the basis of a joint arrangement with each other. Article 15 allows member states in such a case to permit the omission of the parents' figures from consolidation.

UNILEVER

The two parent companies, Unilever N.V. and Unilever PLC, operate as nearly as practicable as a single company, have identical Boards of Directors and are linked by agreements including an Equalisation Agreement which is designed so that the position of the shareholders of both companies is as nearly as possible the same as if they held shares in a single company. The combined affairs of N.V. and PLC are, therefore, more important to shareholders than those of the two separate companies.

Consequently combined accounts are prepared for Unilever N.V. and Unilever PLC which comprise an aggregation of the consolidated accounts of Unilever N.V. and its group companies and the consolidated accounts of Unilever PLC and its group companies.

ROYAL DUTCH/SHELL

The financial statements take the form of an aggregation . . . of the accounts of the companies in which Royal Dutch Petroleum (Royal Dutch) and the Shell Transport and Trading Company, p.l.c. (Shell Transport), either directly or indirectly, have a majority of the voting power or have a majority equity interest . . . The accounts of the above two Parent Companies are not included in the financial statements, whose object is to demonstrate the financial position and results of operations of a group of undertakings in which each Parent Company has an interest in common whilst maintaining its separate identity.

Figure 5.1 Extracts from Annual Reports of Unilever and Shell

Accounting Rules and Formats

The seventh Directive follows the prescriptive approach of the fourth in laying down a number of accounting rules and requiring the use of prescribed formats. Article 16 contains the general provisions which, *mutatis mutandis,* repeat the requirements of Article 2 of the fourth Directive. Consolidated accounts are to comprise a consolidated balance sheet, a consolidated profit and loss account and notes on the accounts. These documents constitute a composite whole. The accounts are to be drawn up clearly and in accordance with the Directive. They must give a true and fair view of the assets, liabilities, financial position and profit or loss of the undertakings included therein taken as a whole. Where application of the provisions of the Directive would not be sufficient to give a true and fair view, additional information must be given. Where in exceptional cases the application of a provision is incompatible with the giving of a true and fair view, that provision must be departed from, with disclosure of the departure, the reasons for it and a statement of its effect. Member states may define the exceptional cases and lay down relevant special rules.

No model formats are given in the Directive. Instead those of the fourth Directive are to apply 'without prejudice to the provisions of this Directive and taking account of the essential adjustments resulting from the particular characteristics of consolidated accounts as compared with annual accounts' (Art. 17). It is expressly provided that, where appropriate, minority interest figures shall be shown as separate headings in the balance sheet and profit and loss account (Art. 21) and that in special circumstances member states may permit the elements of stocks (inventories) to be combined.

The Directive requires global (full) consolidation (Articles 18 and 22), equity accounting is mandatory for associated undertakings (Art. 33), with proportional consolidation as an allowable option for joint ventures (Art. 32). Acquisition (purchase) accounting is implicitly preferred to merger accounting (pooling of interests) but the latter is available as an option (Arts. 19 and 20). Goodwill is to be calculated as at the date of first consolidation (Art. 19), i.e. by the 'Anglo-Saxon' rather than by the French or German methods (Nobes and Parker, 1985, p. 230).

Whatever methods of consolidation are used must be applied consistently (Art. 25). Inter-company debts, transactions and profits must be eliminated (Art. 26). Consolidated accounts are, with some exceptions, to be drawn up as at the same date as the annual accounts of the parent undertaking (Art. 27). Uniform valuation methods are to be used, deferred taxation is to be recognised, and disclosure is to be made of exceptional value adjustments made solely for tax purposes (Art. 29).

Disclosure and Audit

Articles 34 and 36 of the Directive set out a large number of items which must be disclosed in the notes on the accounts and the directors' report. These are largely similar to the requirements of the fourth Directive, adjusted for groups. The audit of consolidated accounts is compulsory. The auditor must also verify that the annual (directors') report is consistent with the consolidated accounts (Art. 37).

5.3 Purposes of the Directive

One of the purposes of a Directive on group accounting is clear: it is that, as for other aspects of accounting, harmonisation should enable easier international comparison of financial statements (whether of multinationals or not) and easier preparation of financial statements for multinationals. However, it is also clear that the EEC's seventh Directive on company law had two additional purposes behind it. First, if harmonisation of practices had been the only aim, the simplest method would have been to have *no* consolidation, for this was the prevailing practice throughout much of the EEC in the mid-1970s when drafting began. Thus, one aim of the seventh Directive was to 'improve' practice by requiring consolidation for all subsidiaries of groups above a certain size. A second aim was particularly apparent in the drafts of the Directive: the disclosure of information to assist in the control of multinationals by host countries. The 'harmonisation' and 'improvement' aims are discussed several times in this chapter. Certainly, when all the provisions outlined above have been brought into effect, they will represent a degree of harmonisation and an increased average level of consolidation.

The 'control' aim of the Directive is far less visible in the adopted version than it was in the drafts of 1976 and 1978. It is clear in these drafts that the Commission had uses in mind for consolidating financial statements additional to the appraisal of groups by shareholders and investors. There were proposals for consolidation by groups under the control of unincorporated businesses, and by EEC companies which were unconnected except for their common control by an undertaking outside the EEC. In the former case, it was suggested by some that the various world-wide commercial interests of the Catholic Church would have to be consolidated because they were controlled by the Pope! In the latter case, a 'horizontal consolidation' would be required from the various EEC subsidiaries of Ford, although none of them owned or controlled any of the others. Which

EEC shareholders or investors would benefit from these consolidations? What would it have to do with harmonisation of accounting? Persistent asking of these questions no doubt helped to remove the mandatory status of these provisions. (Traditionally, governments have not been seen as users of accounts in Anglo-Saxon countries. Governments should be capable of demanding the information they need by disclosure requirements, rather than by extra consolidations. Disclosure of 'related party' transactions is an attempt to satisfy this demand.)

Returning to harmonisation, it should be clear that the aim is not uniformity. Harmonisation can be defined as 'a process of increasing the compatibility of accounting practices by setting bounds to their degree of variation' (Nobes and Parker, 1985, p. 331). It does not imply the imposition of a rigid and narrow set of rules. There is no doubt, however, that the Directive is a major step towards the production by European companies not only of more consolidated statements but also of more comparable ones. It will also have the effect of bringing continental European practice more into line with that of Anglo-Saxon countries.

Nevertheless, the Directive was only adopted as the result of lengthy discussions and a series of compromises, and many options are available to member states. The most important of these options (some of which have already been mentioned) can be summarised as follows:

(a) consolidation may be required where there is *de facto* control even where there is no *de jure* control;
(b) consolidation may be confined to those groups where the parent is a limited company;
(c) financial holding companies may be exempted if certain conditions are met;
(d) small (i.e. both small and medium in fourth Directive terminology) groups may be exempted, except where any of the companies in the group is listed on a stock exchange;
(e) merger accounting may be permitted under certain conditions;
(f) goodwill on consolidation may be written off immediately to reserves rather than amortised;
(g) tax-based valuations need not be eliminated if they are disclosed along with the reasons for them;
(h) the proportional method of consolidation may be required or permitted for joint ventures.

Consolidation practice will also vary within the Community because member states may, if they wish, impose stricter requirements than does the Directive, for example, by calling for more detailed disclosures (Art. 16b).

5.4 Effect of the Directive on Some Major Countries

In this section we discuss in some detail the impact of the Directive on the UK, West Germany and France, and also look briefly at its impact on other EEC countries and some major non-EEC countries.

(i) The United Kingdom

The effect of implementation on UK practice will be quite small. This is because not only is consolidation already well established in the UK but also the Directive has largely followed existing UK practices and because the Companies Act 1981 (now incorporated in the Companies Act 1985) had already adapted the fourth Directive to groups.

There will, however, be many detailed amendments to accounting practice. Likely changes include:

(a) the substitution of voting rights for nominal value in the definition of a subsidiary (Companies Act 1985, Section 736);
(b) the extension of the definition of a subsidiary to include cases where a minority shareholder is able, through a legal agreement, to control a majority of the voting rights (see Section 5.2) (the UK is unlikely to introduce control contracts or to require consolidation where there is a participating interest plus actual dominant influence or unified management);
(c) bringing unincorporated entitities within the scope of consolidation;
(d) fewer sub-group consolidations, because of the exemptions for 90%-owned intermediate parents and for wholly-owned UK sub-groups with EEC (and possibly non-EEC) parents;
(e) minor changes in the rules of merger accounting.

The UK is unlikely to:

(a) require parent undertakings which are not companies to draw up consolidated accounts;
(b) exempt small groups (although these might be allowed to produce group accounts rather than simply consolidated accounts) (Nobes and Parker, 1985, pp. 224–5);
(c) insist on or deny the option of proportional consolidation for joint ventures.

It will become a legal requirement (at least for large companies) to consolidate and not just to prepare group accounts.

Implementation of the seventh Directive will, like that of the fourth, mean that large sections of existing accounting standards (specifically SSAPs 1, 14, 22 and 23) will be incorporated into legislation. This phenomenon, although speeded up by the EEC's programme of company law harmonisation, did not originate with it. The accounting provisions of the Companies Act 1948, the principal Act until 1985, were heavily influenced by the Recommendations on Accounting Principles of the Institute of Chartered Accountants in England and Wales. It may be that many UK companies will have to become more precise with their practices when the traditional UK rules become law. For example, it is widely believed that 'fair value accounting' for a subsidiary's assets (as required by SSAPs 14 and 22) has been honoured more in the breach than the observance for some types of asset.

(ii) West Germany

Although consolidated financial statements are well established in West Germany, implementation of the seventh Directive will, unlike implementation in the UK, have a considerable effect (Brooks and Mertin, 1986). The Federal Republic was, mainly for political reasons, very slow to implement the fourth Directive, but has been very quick in passing the legislation for the seventh. This has been achieved by implementing both Directives, and indeed the eighth (on auditing), in one Accounting Directives Law or *Bilanzrichtlinien-Gesetz* (BiRiLiG). The new law, passed on 19 December 1985, differs from the UK approach in that it mainly amends the Commercial Code, which is applicable to *all* legal forms and sizes of business, by inserting into it a Third Book. (But the rules relating to consolidation apply only to public companies and to other entities if very large: see Table 5.2) The law came into effect on 1 January 1986, but the new rules relating to consolidated financial statements apply only to financial years beginning after 31 December 1989. Companies may apply them earlier if they so wish, but not partially. The new rules are, in general, more extensive but also more flexible than the old.

One very important practical effect of the new law is the lowering of size thresholds. This will greatly increase the number of groups required to consolidate. The old and new limits are shown in Table 5.2. For exemption, a company must not exceed two of the three criteria (balance sheet total, sales, number of employees) for two consecutive years.

Many of the provisions of the Accounting Directives Law have the effect of bringing West German legislation much closer to that pertaining in the UK. These requirements include:

(a) The notes to the accounts are to be much more comprehensive and to form an integral part of the annual financial statements (Arts. 264 (1), 313 and 314).

(b) Consolidations are to be on a world-wide basis, i.e. to include foreign as well as domestic subsidiaries (Art. 294(1)). The inclusion of foreign subsidiaries was formerly voluntary and practised only by the largest companies (Nobes and Parker, 1985, pp. 226–7).

(c) Consolidation is no longer defined exclusively in terms of unified management. A shareholding is now necessary as well. The requirement to consolidate cannot be refuted where there is (i) a majority of voting rights, (ii) controlling personal influence, (iii) a control contract, or (iv) a controlling influence based on a by-law provision (Art. 290). These new requirements are unlikely greatly to increase the scope of consolidation in practice.

(d) Deferred taxation is to be recognised (whether a liability or an asset) (Art. 306). Deferred tax has not previously been recognised in German financial statements. In a country where accounting profit is often identical to taxable income (Nobes and Parker, 1985, p. 105), deferred tax is less important than in the UK or USA, except of course for non-German subsidiaries.

(e) Goodwill is to be calculated as at the date of acquisition or first consolidation, not every year. Fair values, not historical costs of subsidiaries' assets, are to be used (Art. 301). This marks the abandonment of the German practice of calculating a new 'consolidation difference' every year.

(f) The equity method is mandatory for associated undertakings (Art. 311), although proportional consolidation is permitted but not required for joint ventures (Art. 310). Under the previous legislation neither the equity method nor proportional consolidation were permitted.

(g) Unrealised inter-company losses (as well as profits) must be eliminated (Art. 304).

(h) Consolidated statements are to show a true and fair view: '*ein den tatsächlichen Verhältnissen entschprechendes Bild*' (Art. 297(2)). The requirement of a true and fair view is new to West German law. It is unlikely to make much difference to accounting practice (Busse von Colbe, 1984).

(i) There will be clearer and more understandable balance sheet and profit and loss account formats, with disclosure of minority interests within the equity section of the consolidated balance sheet and in the profit and loss account (Art. 307). Standardised formats have long been established in West German law and practice. The UK influence here has been to make them more 'user-friendly'.

(j) Individual financial statements of entities consolidated must conform to the accounting principles and valuation methods and formats of the parent in accordance with the 'one entity theory' (Art. 297(3)). This is new to West German law. The previous practice was to keep the accounting principles and valuation methods of the subsidiaries unchanged.

(k) Sub-groups of EEC parents are, subject to certain conditions, to be exempt from preparing consolidated accounts (Art. 291).

(l) Merger accounting (pooling of interests) is allowable under certain conditions (Art. 302).

(iii) France

Implementation of the seventh Directive will also have a considerable effect on French law and accounting practice. The Directive has been largely implemented by the Law 85–11 of 3 January 1985, the Decree 86–221 of 17 February 1986 and an addition to the national accounting plan.

As in West Germany, there is likely to be a greatly increased number of consolidations from 1990 onwards (when consolidations will be required of all groups above a certain size), although small groups will be exempted. In the past French companies have been, by Anglo-Saxon standards, slow to publish consolidated statements. Even in 1983 only about 75% of *listed* companies published consolidated accounts and they were not legally obliged to do so until 1986 (Law, 357–1, 357–2)[1]. What size limits will be chosen for small groups is not yet known but it is possible that the limits will approach those of the smallest listed companies.

Exemption is also granted to 'wholly-owned' sub-groups so long as the accounts of the group to which they belong are prepared in accordance with the seventh Directive or in an equivalent manner, are subject to an independent audit, and are available to the sub-group shareholders (with an accompanying translation if they are not in French). The Decree lists the minimum requirements for equivalence (Law 357–2, Decree 248–13).

---

[1] All references are to the Law of 24 July 1966 as amended and to the Decree of 23 March 1967 as amended. Unlike the practice in the UK, changes in French laws and decrees are inserted immediately into existing legislation.

Subsidiaries must be excluded from consolidation if control is subject to severe long-term restrictions, and may be excluded on the grounds of shareholdings held for sale only, of immateriality, or of inability to obtain necessary information without undue cost or delay (Law 357–4).

Whereas the published financial statements of parent companies in France have been notable for their uniformity, consolidated statements have shown great diversity. A report by the Conseil National de la Comptabilité (National Accounting Council), first issued in 1968 and revised in 1978, has been very influential but it has not been followed in all its details. Several multinational companies, especially those which have sought finance on international markets, have adopted Anglo-Saxon principles of consolidation. The effect of implementation of the seventh Directive will be both to decrease diversity and to strengthen the move towards Anglo-Saxon type consolidations. Consolidated statements will however be less rigidly regulated than non-consolidated ones. One example of this is that, whereas parent company balance sheets must be horizontal in form, consolidated balance sheets can be either horizontal or vertical (Decree 248–9).

Until recently not all French consolidated financial statements were audited. Legislation (Law 228) now provides that where such statements are published, *commissaires aux comptes* (state registered auditors) must certify that they are 'regular' (i.e. in accordance with the regulations) and 'sincere', and give a true and fair view. They must also verify that the attached directors' report is 'sincere' and that the information in it is in agreement with the financial statements. The requirement for published accounts to give a true and fair view (*image fidèle*) is recent in France and dates only from the implementation of the fourth Directive (Nobes and Parker, 1985, pp. 81–2).

French legislation (Law 357–3, Decreee 248) distinguishes clearly between global consolidation, proportional consolidation and the equity method (*mise en équivalence*). The first method is to be used for undertakings under the exclusive control of the consolidating company; the second for those controlled jointly; and the third for those over which a significant influence is exercised. This follows the common (but not previously universal) practice in France of applying proportional consolidation to joint ventures, rather than, as is normal in the UK and USA, using the equity method. Another notable departure from UK practice is the presumption of exclusive control where more than *40 per cent* of the voting rights are held and no other shareholder has a larger shareholding. Significant influence is presumed where more than 20 per cent of the voting rights are held (Law 357–1).

In the past, French companies have dealt in a number of different ways with 'differences on consolidation' and have not always calculated a goodwill on consolidation figure. Nor have they, given the very close relationships between accounting profit and taxable income, accounted for deferred taxation. In future goodwill is to be calculated at the date of first consolidation and duly amortised (Decree 248–3) and deferred taxation (e.g. that of foreign subsidiaries) is to be recognised (Decree 248–11).

Both the fourth and seventh Directives have greatly increased the importance in French annual reports of the notes (*annexe*) in which much information previously unavailable will now be reported. The main items are listed in Article 248–12 of the Decree.

(iv) The Netherlands

Full implementation of the seventh Directive had not yet taken place (in 1987) in the Netherlands but it will have little practical effect since consolidations are already well established, and partial implementation was achieved at the same time as implementation of the fourth Directive. It will, however, be necessary to provide a more detailed legal definition of what constitutes a subsidiary undertaking, and consolidations rather than simply group accounts will become mandatory. On the other hand fewer sub-group consolidations will be required. Exemption for such groups with non-EEC parents raises the problem of 'equivalence'. This is because consolidated financial statements prepared in conformity with international accounting standards had been, by ministerial decree, recognised as equivalent (*IASC News*, April 1986); whereas the EEC Commission opposes this. Implementation of the Directive will also bring minor changes in disclosure requirements. Small groups are unlikely to be exempted from consolidation.

(v) Other EEC Countries

Consolidations are still rare in Greece, Italy, Luxembourg, Portugal and Spain, and the seventh Directive will bring major changes. Full advantage is likely to be taken of the small groups exemption, since otherwise the relatively underdeveloped accountancy professions in these countries would be unable to cope. Belgium has already implemented much of the seventh Directive and consolidation is increasingly common. Consolidation is also common in Denmark, where implementation is likely to make practice less diverse and the equity method more usual. Irish practice is very close to British.

(vi) Non-EEC Countries

Although of no direct effect, the seventh Directive is likely to influence the laws of such other European countries such as Austria, Finland, Norway, Switzerland and Sweden.

The influence of the EEC Directives is likely to be particularly great in Switzerland where discussions are underway concerning how to introduce accounting regulations more akin to those existing in other developed, industrialised countries. In 1983, the Swiss government submitted the draft of a new company law to parliament which *inter alia* makes consolidated accounts compulsory wherever two or more companies are managed on a unified basis. There are no proposed requirements on consolidation techniques. A Foundation for Accounting and Reporting Recommendations was created in 1984 and has issued non-mandatory guidelines on consolidated statements.

The above laws and guidelines have been influenced by practice outside Switzerland, especially that in the USA and major EEC countries. A more direct influence arises from the fact that Swiss multinational companies have important subsidiaries within the EEC which are themselves parents of sub-groups. As already noted, EEC member states may exempt these sub-groups from consolidation if the parent (Swiss) undertaking prepares consolidated statements in accordance with the seventh Directive or in a manner equivalent.

Faced with this rule Swiss parent companies with EEC subsidiaries have the options of acceptance, avoidance or applying for exemption (Zünd, 1988). The last is the most popular and will encourage consolidation in Switzerland. The definition of 'equivalence' is vital, however, since few Swiss companies are likely to be willing to accept the provisions of the Directive in their entirety. Some Swiss companies are likely to prove willing to prepare sub-consolidations. Avoidance by restructuring the sub-group hardly seems worthwhile.

The seventh Directive will have a similar direct impact on Swedish multinationals which also have important subsidiaries in EEC countries. The difference is that consolidation is already firmly established in Sweden, so that equivalence may be more easily granted, although it should be noted that because of legal doubts the equity method, mandatory in the seventh Directive, is not universally accepted (Cooke, 1988). The indirect impact of the Directive itself is likely to be less, since the main external influences on the consolidation practices of Swedish multinationals are American and British.

The seventh Directive will have little or no effect on the laws of USA, Japan, Australia and Canada, although it will, of course, help to bring European practice closer to that prevailing in other parts of the world. US, Japanese, Australian and Canadian groups with subsidiaries in the EEC will face similar problems regarding 'equivalence' to those of Swiss and Swedish companies.

5.5 Problem Areas

Goodwill (Difference on Consolidation)

A difference arises on consolidation where the amount paid by the investor company is greater or less than its share of the tangible and identifiable intangible net assets of the investee. The treatment of this difference has varied considerably from country to country. For example, in the UK, except where merger accounting is used, the calculation is made at the date of acquisition, taking the net assets of the subsidiary at their fair value. The balancing figure (termed 'goodwill on consolidation') is normally positive and is usually written off immediately against reserves, although the relevant accounting standard (SSAP 22) also allows capitalisation followed by amortisation over the economic life. Negative goodwill on consolidation is credited to reserves. In the USA, apart from poolings of interests, practice is the same as in the UK except that positive goodwill must be amortised over a period of not more than 40 years and negative goodwill must be allocated proportionately against the fair values of fixed assets other than investments. Pooling of interests in the USA is more common than its equivalent, merger accounting, is in the UK. Dutch practice is much the same as that in the UK except that there is no merger accounting.

The seventh Directive covers goodwill in the rather obscurely worded Article 19. This article is broadly based on Anglo-Saxon practice. It appears to require the use of fair values rather than book values, and the calculation to be made at the date of first consolidation (not necessarily the same as the date of acquisition). Book values can be retained in the subsidiary's own accounts. The article does not deal with the calculation of goodwill when a subsidiary is not wholly owned.

Article 30 of the Directive allows either immediate write-off or amortisation of positive goodwill but not the carrying of unamortised goodwill as a permanent asset. Negative goodwill that arises as a result of expected unfavourable future costs can be credited to profit and loss when those expectations are fulfilled. Negative goodwill arising from a bargain purchase can be transferred to profit and loss account on realisation.

The treatment of consolidation differences that was previously used in West Germany and France does not comply with the Directive. In the former it has been the normal practice to calculate the difference *at the date of each balance sheet*, using the book value of the investee. This book value was defined as the sum of the investee's share capital and reserves according to its own books. The reserves excluded the profit or loss for the current year except to the extent that transfers had been made to or from reserves. The usual French method was the same, except that the book value did not include any part of the profit or loss for the year. These methods meant that the size of the difference varied from year to year and was a mixture of goodwill, undervaluation of assets and post-acquisition profits. Some companies split the difference into debit and credit portions. In any case there was some diversity of practice.

Both countries are now moving much closer to UK and US practice. In West Germany, on first consolidation, companies may use either the 'book value method' or the 'purchase method' (Accounting Directives Law, Art. 301). Under the former method the book values (adjusted if necessary to the parent's accounting principles) of a subsidiary's net assets are compared with the carrying value of the investment in the parent's books. If a difference arises this must be added to or subtracted from the relevant balance sheet headings. Under the latter method, the book values are replaced by market values. The revalued net assets of the subsidiary must not, however, exceed the cost of the investment. Credit differences cannot therefore arise under the purchase method. Debit differences still remaining are recorded in the consolidated balance sheet as goodwill and amortised in subsequent balance sheets (Art. 309). Pooling of interests is allowed under Article 302 which provides for any difference arising to be deducted from or added to reserves.

The French rules are contained in the national accounting plan. A difference on first consolidation (*écart de première consolidation*) is calculated as the difference between the cost of acquisition and the net assets acquired (adjusted if necessary to accord with group accounting policies). Any part of the difference not needed to revalue the separable assets of the subsidiary is treated as either positive goodwill (*prime d'acquisition*), an asset to be carried in the consolidated balance sheet and amortised, or as negative goodwill, which is usually to be included under 'provisions for liabilities and charges'. The logic of this treatment is that negative goodwill corresponds either to a provision for loss or to a potential capital gain arising from a bargain purchase. Positive goodwill is amortised over a period which reasonably reflects its expected economic life at the date of acquisition. Negative goodwill can be credited periodically to profit and loss account.

The effect of the seventh Directive will be to bring practices in this area closer together, largely using the Anglo-Saxon rather than the continental European model. There will still be some diversity, however, and EEC practices will still be rather different from American.

Associated Undertakings

The accounting treatment of investments in associated undertakings has also varied from country to country. For example, it has been standard practice in the UK to use the equity method in the consolidated (but not the parent) statements, although unincorporated joint ventures are proportionately consolidated by a few companies. Since the investment is valued at cost plus a share of the associated undertaking's post-acquisition undistributed profits, it includes payment for goodwill. The amount of this goodwill element, where not written off immediately, is separately disclosed in the notes.

In West Germany neither the equity method nor proportional consolidation were allowed before implementation of the seventh Directive. The new law prescribes the equity method, and permits proportional consolidation for joint ventures (Accounting Directives Law, Articles 310–312). At the date of acquisition, shares in associated undertakings may not be shown in the consolidated balance sheet at an amount in excess of their purchase cost. In subsequent years this amount is increased or decreased by the parent's share of the associated undertaking's undistributed profits. Any goodwill arising is treated in the same way as for subsidiaries.

In France, on the other hand, both the equity method and proportional consolidation were in widespread use before the seventh Directive. What was lacking was uniformity in their application. As already noted, the new French legislation prescribes proportional consolidation for joint ventures and the equity method for other associated undertakings. The national accounting plan extends the general rules of consolidation to the equity method, but allows a certain amount of flexibility in their application, given the difficulty and cost of obtaining the necessary information. Goodwill is treated in the same way as for subsidiaries.

In the Netherlands the equity method is used in both the parent and the consolidated statements, with proportional consolidation common but not universal for joint ventures. Since use of the latter form of consolidation in this way is expressly allowed in the Directive, Dutch practice is unlikely to change.

5.6 Summary

The more complex the accounting topic, the more scope there is for international variation. Consolidation can be very complex indeed, particularly in MNEs when foreign subsidiaries and currencies are involved. Consequently, this area exhibits great variety: *from* complete lack of consolidation in some countries *to* the use of four methods within a single company in others; *from* goodwill calculated at fair values at the date of acquisition *to* 'differences on consolidation' calculated on book values once a year; *from* the exclusion of foreign subsidiaries and all associates *to* the full consolidation of even minority-held companies. Furthermore, it is an area where the EEC Commission's harmonisation objectives are particularly ambitious, involving an attempt to do away with the above differences and many others. The mechanism for this task is the seventh Directive on company law.

This chapter has examined the main topics of difference: the nature of a group, the exemptions and exclusions, technical rules, disclosures and audit. The Directive has been seen to have 'improving' and 'controlling', as well as 'harmonising', aims. As a result of the scale of differences, political compromises have led to many options entailing some continued diversity, particularly by exemption of many small groups in some countries.

Actual or proposed measures have been discussed in some detail for the UK, West Germany, and France, with reference also to the effect of the Directive on other EEC and non-EEC countries. The conclusions have been that the effect on UK *law* will be quite substantial although *practice* may change only slightly; that in West Germany and France consolidation will be extended beyond the restricted number of very large companies, and that many Anglo-American practices will become standard; and that in some other countries the change will be even more severe because consolidation has been rare and has only recently arrived.

Lastly, the chapter has discussed the technical areas of goodwill and associates, noting some of the detail of the differences in the late 1980s that will be reduced by the Directive's implementation.

References

Brooks, J.P. and Mertin, D. (1986) *Neues deutsches Bilanzrecht: New German Accounting Legislation*, IDW-Verlag, Düsseldorf.

Busse von Colbe, W. (1984) 'A true and fair view: a German perspective', in S.J. Gray and A.G. Coenenberg (eds) *EEC Accounting Harmonisation: Implementation and Impact of the Fourth Directive*, North Holland.

Cooke, T.E. (1988) *European Financial Reporting: Sweden*, Institute of Chartered Accountants in England and Wales, London.

Nobes, C.W. and Parker, R.H. (1985) *Comparative International Accounting*, 2nd edn, Philip Allan.

Zünd, A. (1988) 'Switzerland and the Seventh Directive', in S.J. Gray and A.G. Coenenberg (eds), *International Group Accounting*, Croom Helm.

Further Reading

Biener, H. (1986) *Die Gesellschafts- und Bilanzrichtlinien-Gesetze nach Änderung durch das Bilanzrichtlinien-Gesetz, BiRiLiG*, Bundesanzeiger, Cologne.

Busse von Colbe, W. and Ordelheide, G. (1984, 5th ed.) *Konzernabschlüsse*, Gabler, Wiesbaden.

Ernst and Whinney (1984) *The Impact of the Seventh Directive*, Financial Times Business Information, London.

Gray, S.J. and Coenenberg, A.G. (1988) *International Group Accounting*, Croom Helm.

McKinnon, S.M. (1984) *The Seventh Directive: Consolidated Accounts in the EEC*, Kluwer Publishing and Arthur Young International.
Nobes, C.W. (1986) 'Financial reporting by multinational groups: a few of the questions and fewer answers', in *Symposium on International Financial Accounting Research*, School of Financial Studies, University of Glasgow.
Organisation for Economic Co-operation and Development (1987) *Consolidation Policies in OECD Countries*, OECD, Paris.
Peat, Marwick, Mitchell & Co. (1984) *Consolidated Accounts: Seventh Directive*.
Raffegau, J. Dufils, P. and Corre, J. (1984) *Les Comptes Consolidés*, Editions Francis Lefebvre, Paris.

6
Segmental Reporting

CLARE B. ROBERTS
SIDNEY J. GRAY

6.1 The Need for Segmental Information

In recent times it has become evident that many companies have grown very much larger and more diversified, both internationally and industrially, and that, allied to this, western economies have become increasingly dependent upon the activities of a few very large companies (see, for example, Stopford, 1983; Stopford and Dunning, 1983).

The size and relative importance of diversified companies has, in turn, presented many problems for the users of accounts. Shareholders are interested in the future cash flows they may obtain from investing in a company and the risk or uncertainty of those cash flows. They are therefore interested in the performance of a company as a whole rather than the performance of any specific part of a company. However, this does not mean that only consolidated information is of value to them. Both the size and uncertainty of future cash flows are likely to be affected by many factors including those that are related to the industries and countries that a company operates in. Different industries and different countries have various profit potentials, degrees and types of risk, and growth opportunities. Different rates of return on investment and different capital needs are also likely to occur across the various segments of a business. Because of this diversification of operations, there has been a demand for companies also to report key disaggregated information, especially turnover and profits. Such disaggregated or segmental data is typically provided for both geographical areas and lines of business.

Segmental information is likely to aid shareholders by allowing them to combine company-specific information with external information and so allow a more accurate assessment of both the risk and potential for future growth. In addition, an idea of the success of past operations can be gained by comparing a company with others, i.e. whether or not a company has done better than other similar companies. However, for most diversified companies such external yardsticks are not available. In principle, the provision of disaggregated data may allow shareholders to compare the success of individual segments with those of other companies. However, given the very large degree of latitude that companies have in deciding upon what constitutes a reportable segment, such an advantage of comparability may be more apparent than real. This is especially the case when comparing profit measures, as not only is there discretion in the choice of segments but also discretion in the methods used for common cost allocations and transfer pricing.

Other users often have a direct relationship not with the company as a whole, but with a part of the company. Disaggregated data regarding the performance of that segment of the company would then be relevant. This would apply to employees, creditors and host governments. All of these groups are likely to be interested, therefore, not only in a company as a whole but also in that sector of a company that most affects themselves. They will often require information that is even more disaggregated than that currently provided. For example, employees will also want information at the plant level, host governments at the individual country level and creditors at the level of the individual subsidiary or legal entity. However, segmentally disaggregated information will go at least some way towards meeting these information needs. This is especially important for those groups such as employees and developing country host governments who often lack the power to demand specific information that is of relevance to themselves in particular.

We will examine the benefits and costs of segmental reporting after a review of the rules and practice.

6.2 The Rules

UK Requirements

It was in 1965 that the first UK requirements for segmental disclosures were introduced: in the Stock Exchange listing requirements. These call for segment disclosure by all quoted companies: turnover and profits by line of business (LOB) segments, and turnover by geographical segments. Profit is also required by geographical segment if contributions are abnormal, that is if the profit rate of a particular segment differs from the average of the whole company. The listing requirements do not have the force of law but compliance is necessary if a company is to maintain its listing.

The requirements for LOB disclosures were reinforced by the 1967 Companies Act. This Act was based partly upon the Jenkins Committee

Report (1962) although it went beyond their recommendations in the area of segmental disclosures. The Act required disclosure in the Directors' Report of the proportion of turnover, and the extent or approximate extent of the contribution to profits, of industry or LOB segments. This applied to all companies carrying on two or more classes of business that in the opinion of the directors differed substantially from each other. The government did not publicly consider the introduction of requirements for geographical segment information until ten years later. In 1977 the then Labour government issued a consultative document, *The Future of Company Reports* (HMSO, 1977a). The objective of this document was to set out the government's views on specific proposals for additional items of disclosure in annual reports. The document recognised that the traditional view of the function of reporting, as being to satisfy the stewardship function only, was increasingly under attack. Instead it accepted many of the wider demands for information and the entity view of corporations that has been recognised in such reports as those by the CBI (1963), the Bullock Committee (HMSO, 1977b) and the Accounting Standards Committee (1975).

The 1977 consultative document recognised that the 1967 Act's segmental requirements contained two serious weaknesses. Firstly, the information was provided in the Directors' Report and so was not subject to audit. Secondly, it left too much to the discretion of the directors in deciding what constituted a significant, and thus reportable, segment. The document proposed instead that segmental information should be disclosed in the notes to the accounts and should include turnover, profit, capital employed and the number of employees both by line of business and geographical area. Any accounting problems and the definition of what constituted a reportable segment were to be left to the accountancy profession to develop in an SSAP. However, possibly as a result of a change of government, these proposals were not acted upon.

The next legislation in the area was the 1981 Companies Act which implemented the EEC fourth Directive. The Companies Act (now the 1985 Act which includes the provisions of the 1981 Act) requires the disclosure of geographically segmented turnover, whilst for line of business information it demands disclosure of both turnover and profit before tax. The Act also states that if any market or class of business is immaterial (a term not defined) it may be combined with another. Even more discretion is given to companies by the additional statement that 'if disclosure is seriously prejudicial to the interests of the company that information need not be disclosed' (Schedule 4, para. 55(5)), it being sufficient instead to state that such disclosures have not been made. The only help the Act provides regarding segment identification is the statement that 'the directors of the company should have regard to the manner in which the company's activities are organised' (para. 55(3)).

The most important new requirement was that such information should be provided in the notes to the accounts so that for the first time it had to be audited. However, the Act still fails to tackle the more serious problem of segment identification: there are no definitions of what is material or what a reportable segment is, so that a possible consequence of this is either lack of disclosure or misleading disclosures. Emmanuel and Gray (1977) have shown that leaving this to the discretion of management has led to disclosures by many large UK companies that are either inadequate or inconsistent. Even if such discretion does not encourage deliberate manipulation, 'no amount of sophisticated data can remedy the damage caused by segments wrongly identified in the first place' (Emmanuel and Gray, 1977, p. 37). The only guidance in the UK on what constitutes a reportable segment is provided by the Stock Exchange guidance notes which require disclosure of revenues by geographical areas if foreign operations account for at least 10 per cent of total revenues. Such disclosures should be on a continental basis unless one continent accounts for more than 50 per cent of all revenues, in which case a finer classification should be employed.

US Requirements

The UK requirements can be compared with those in the USA, the country that has the most extensive requirements in this area. In August 1969 the SEC required the disclosure of line of business information in registration documents and, a year later, extended this to include similar disclosures in the annual Form 10-K (Buckley, Buckley and Plank, 1980). The requirement called for 5 years' information on total sales or revenue, income before tax and extraordinary items. In addition, if a company has 'material operations' overseas this should also be disclosed and also, where practicable, the volume and relative profitability (Form 10-K, para. C.2.d). In January 1974 these requirements were extended, such that the information also had to be included in the annual reports of companies that file accounts with the SEC.

The requirements began to cover all quoted companies when SFAS 14 was issued (FASB, December 1976). This requires, for both line of business and geographical segments, disclosure of revenue from unaffiliated customers, intra-group transfers, operating profit or loss or net income, or other profitability measures and identifiable assets. In addition, for industry segments, companies must also disclose depreciation, capital expenditure and equity in the net income and assets of associates (see Table 6.1 for an example). The requirement to disclose segmented assets adds an extra dimension, compared to the UK rules.

Table 6.1 Company X: Information about the Company's Operations in Different Industries, Year Ended 31 December 19XX ($)

	Industry A	*Industry B*	*Industry C*	*Other Industries*	*Adjustments and Eliminations*	*Consolidated*
Sales to affiliated customers	1,000	2,000	1,500	200		4,700
Intersegment sales	200	—	500	—	(700)	—
Total revenue	1,200	2,000	2,000	200	(700)	4,700
Operating profit	200	290	600	50	(40)	1,100
Equity in net income of Company Z						100
General corporate expenses						(100)
Interest expense						(200)
Income from continuing operations before income taxes						900
Identifiable assets at 31 December 19XX	2,000	4,050	6,000	1,000	(50)	13,000
Investment in net assets of Company Z						400
Corporate assets						1,600
Total assets at 31 December 19XX						15,000

Source: FASB, 1976.

These requirements do not provide a clear definition of identifiable segments. For example, SFAS 14 states that:

> foreign geographical areas are individual countries or groups of countries as may be determined to be appropriate in an enterprise's particular circumstances. Factors to be considered include proximity, economic affinity, similarities in business environments and the nature, scale and degree of interrelationship of the enterprise's operations in the various countries (Para. 34).

Even less clear guidance is provided for determining what constitutes an identifiable line of business segment:

> No single set of characteristics is universally applicable in determining the industry segments of all enterprises, nor is any single characteristic determinative in all cases. Consequently determination of an enterprise's industry segments must depend to a considerable extent on the judgement of the management of the enterprise (Para. 12).

Once the segments have been identified, clear guidance is given as to what constitutes a reportable segment. For geographical segments, these should be reported if segment sales account for at least 10 per cent of total sales or if identifiable assets account for at least 10 per cent of total identifiable assets. Similarly, line of business segments should be separately disclosed if either of these requirements are met or if segment profits/losses account for at least 10 per cent of the profits/losses of all segments that incurred a profit or loss respectively.

Many other countries also require segmental information. In particular, the requirements in Canada (CICA Accounting Regulations, Section 1700, April 1979) and Australia (AARF, March 1984) both have requirements similar to those in the USA. The current UK requirements are a direct outcome of the EEC fourth Directive, and so such requirements also apply to most of the other EEC countries, although as yet not all countries have legislated for the fourth Directive (Oldham, 1987).

The IASC

Although the accountancy profession in the UK is only now investigating this issue, the IASC has issued a standard (IAS 14, October 1981) which follows fairly closely the requirements in the USA. Thus it requires (for both line of business and geographical segments) information on turnover, with internal and external revenues shown separately, operating results and identifiable assets, in either absolute or relative terms, plus a reconciliation statement. The requirement applies to all quoted companies that provide consolidated statements. However, in practice, many of the requirements are very seldom met by UK companies.

The OECD

Other important influences on the disclosures made by companies may be codes of conduct, especially those issued by the OECD and the UN, although they have no legal backing, being voluntary codes of 'good conduct' only. The OECD guidelines (OECD, 1976) call for the disclosure of the geographical areas where operations are carried out and the principal activities in each area, plus geographical disclosures of turnover, operating results, significant new capital investment and the average number of employees. After receiving comments on the guidelines a review was issued (OECD, 1979). This stated that:

> Problems were also raised with respect to segmentation of information. In particular a number of companies expressed doubts as to whether disclosure by 'geographical area' was always the most appropriate method of segmentation. These problems of geographical breakdown should, however, not be exaggerated . . . It has to be emphasised, however, that the Guidelines reflect the value member governments place on geographical segmentation of information (Para. 48d).

For LOB disclosures the code calls for information on turnover and, if practicable, significant new capital investments.

The United Nations

In 1976 the UN set up the Group of Experts on International Standards of Accounting and Reporting and charged them with preparing a list of items of both financial and non-financial information that should be issued, as a minimum, in general purpose reports, both at the level of the group as a whole and for the individual member company. This group reported in 1977 (UN, 1977). They called for the disclosure of geographical and LOB information on external sales, internal transfers, operating results and, to the extent identifiable, either total assets and net assets or total assets and total liabilities, with at least separate identification of gross property, plant and equipment, accumulated depreciation and long-term assets. They also called for the disclosure of investments, the principal activities, the basis of accounting for transfers, the total number of employees and, for geographical areas, a description of any exposures to exceptional risks (pp. 66–7 and p. 76). In 1982 the UN issued a report listing the items agreed upon so far (UN, 1982). This stated that the disclosure of information by geographical and LOB segments in respect of turnover had been agreed upon, and that there 'may be circumstances' where companies should disclose significant new investments in land, buildings, plant and equipment and the average number of employees. They had still failed to reach agreement upon whether or not the other items recommended should be reported.

6.3 The Content of Disclosures

There is relatively little empirical evidence available regarding the incidence of segmental disclosures or the actual practices of companies. Currently the only survey regarding the position for UK companies after the 1981 Companies Act is that of the ICAEW (1986). This compares the number of companies disclosing segmental profits and turnover in the years 1981–2 and 1983–4 (see Table 6.2) but provides no information on other segmental information or the number and types of segments disclosed. From Table 6.2 it appears that the legal requirements led many companies, especially medium sized and large unlisted companies, to disclose *less* information, in particular regarding geographical segment profits. Whether it has led to a decrease in other voluntary disclosures in this area has still to be investigated.

Gray and Radebaugh (1984) also provide limited evidence that more detailed legislation may have the effect of actually reducing the amount of information disclosed. They compare the geographical segment information provided by 58 US and 35 UK companies in 1979. The US companies disclosed between 3 and 6 segments, with an average of 4 segments, whilst the UK companies, faced with very much less detailed rules on segment identification and the amount of information they must disclose, reported between 3 and 9 segments, with an average of 6 segments. However, the only information that was more prevalent in the UK reports was employee information (37 per cent versus 10 per cent for the US sample).

Table 6.2 Segmental Disclosures: Items Disclosed by Size of Company

	Large Listed		*Medium Listed*		*Large Unlisted*		*Total*	
	'83–4	*'81–2*	*'83–4*	*'81–2*	*'83–4*	*'81–2*	*'83–4*	*'81–2*
No. of companies	100	100	150	150	50	50	300	300
Turnover (%)								
by activity	89	88	73	64	48	42	74	68
geographically	85	86	65	66	40	12	68	63
Profit (%)								
by activity	88	83	63	60	24	34	65	63
geographically	51	59	21	46	2	10	28	44
No segmental disclosures	6	2	15	15	40	50	16	17

Source: ICAEW *Financial Reporting* 1985–86, p. 158.

6.4 The Problems of Segmental Disclosures

Segmental information now has to be audited both in the UK and in the USA, and this presents a problem regarding the verifiability of the information. Particular problems here are those of common cost allocations and intra-group transfers, and so transfer pricing. Whilst these problems mean that the information may not be as verifiable as some other items of financial information, a trade-off between verifiability and relevance is required.

Another problem facing the auditor is that of segment identification. In the absence of clear guidelines the task of the auditor in assessing whether the segments disclosed are reasonable must be a very difficult one. As described above, the Companies Act 1985 leaves segment identification to the discretion of the directors of each company, on the grounds that what is relevant and reportable will depend upon the unique characteristics of each company. The FASB instead provides detailed and prescriptive rules regarding what constitutes a reportable segment. However, again the decision on what constitutes an identifiable segment, and so potentially reportable, is very largely left up to the discretion of each company.

Arnold, Holder and Mann (1980) provide some evidence regarding the types of geographical segments reported by US companies. They examined 200 10-K reports for 1978, 131 of which had reported geographical segments. These disclosures were classified into six types: (i) country (ii) subcontinent (iii) continent (iv) global (v) other as a specific segment (vi) unique (e.g. Americas and Australia). Of these 131 companies, only 47 reported segments that fell into only one category, as shown in Table 6.3. The remaining 84 companies used multiple classifications as shown in Table 6.4. This demonstrates that there is quite considerable diversity in practice with respect to the choice of segments.

Emmanuel and Gray (1977) examined the segmental disclosures made by 100 UK companies in 1975/6. Of these, 78 disclosed LOB data. However, in only 35 of these cases were the data consistent with the supplementary information provided. Of the 87 that disclosed geographical information only, 27 were consistent with either the chairman's or directors' report and

Table 6.3 Companies Reporting Single Category Segments

	Number	*Percentage*
Country	11	23.4
Subcontinent	2	4.2
Continent	2	4.2
Global	32	68.2
	47	100.0

Table 6.4 Companies Reporting Multiple Classified Segments

	Companies		*Disclosures*
	Number	*Percentage*	*Percentage*
Country	33	39.3	16.3
Subcontinent	36	42.9	17.7
Continent	47	56.0	23.2
Other	63	75.0	31.0
Unique	24	28.6	11.8
			100.0

15 were consistent with the grouping of the subsidiaries. They concluded that, overall, the disclosures appeared to reflect inadequately either the scope of business or the international operations of these companies. Although these two studies are now old there appears to be no reason to believe that the situation has changed.

This lack of guidance regarding segment identification implies that the advantage of comparability across companies has been sacrificed in favour of relevance and the provision of the most useful information for each company. However, it also means that companies are able to manipulate disclosures in order to present the best possible picture of their operations. For example, they can hide the poor performance of one area of their operations by aggregating it with another that has done particularly well. The apparent lack of consistency in the disclosures appears to suggest that comparability of information has been sacrificed for an advantage that may be much more apparent than real.

As shown above, companies are required to disclose both industry and

Table 6.5 BOC Group — Notes on Financial Statements: Segmental Information

(a) Turnover by business – 1986 *Turnover by region of origin*

	Europe[1]	*Africa*	*Americas*[2]	*Asia/ Pacific*	*1986 Total*
	£ million	*£ million*	*£ million*	*£ million*	*£ million*
Gases and related products	290.7	121.4	423.7	559.4	1,395.2
Health care	122.1	38.1	321.7	34.9	516.8
Carbon and carbide	16.8	—	152.3	—	169.1
Special products and services	110.3	14.8	42.5	24.6	192.2
Continuing businesses	539.9	174.3	940.2	618.9	2,273.3

Table 6.5 (continued)

	Europe[1] £ million	*Africa* £ million	*Americas*[2] £ million	*Asia/ Pacific* £ million	*1986 Total* £ million
Discontinued businesses	—	—	95.4	1.9	97.3
Turnover, including related companies	539.9	174.3	1,035.6	620.8	2,370.6
Less turnover of related companies					
BOC Group share	10.3	11.5	2.5	176.3	200.6
External share	10.2	15.0	2.4	197.8	225.4
Turnover	519.4	147.8	1,030.7	246.7	1,944.6
Turnover by destination (customer location)	505.6	154.1	994.3	290.6	1,944.6
Turnover by business – 1985					*1985*
Gases and related products	266.9	108.8	438.8	511.6	1,326.1
Health care	109.1	24.2	288.7	31.9	453.9
Carbon and carbide	16.4	—	152.7	—	169.1
Special products and services	90.9	13.4	35.6	24.3	164.2
Continuing businesses	483.3	146.4	915.8	567.8	2,113.3
Discontinued businesses	4.7	—	143.2	0.2	148.1
Turnover, including related companies	488.0	146.4	1,059.0	568.0	2,261.4
Less turnover of related companies					
BOC Group share	8.1	11.9	—	137.1	157.1
External share	8.1	19.9	—	175.4	203.4
Turnover	471.8	114.6	1,059.0	255.5	1,900.9
Turnover by destination (customer location)	462.2	118.4	1,032.8	287.5	1,900.9

(b) Profit, capital employed and capital expenditure

	Operating profit		*Capital employed*		*Capital expenditure*	
	1986 £ million	*1985* £ million	*1986* £ million	*1985* £ million	*1986* £ million	*1985* £ million
(i) Regional analysis						
Europe	66.6	68.7	508.4	456.5	109.4	113.9
Africa	24.6	15.8	71.6	107.2	10.5	9.5
Americas	115.3	110.1	809.7	1,060.8	87.4	91.2
Asia/Pacific	53.3	41.1	320.7	307.8	26.7	20.9
Continuing businesses	259.8	235.7	1,710.4	1,932.3	234.0	235.5
(ii) Business analysis						
Gases and related products	160.5	156.3	1,174.1	1,189.1	157.3	154.6
Health care	88.5	73.2	278.5	270.8	32.4	29.7
Carbon and carbide	0.1	(6.8)	213.2	402.6	4.2	18.2
Special products and services	24.3	20.5	111.2	87.1	33.5	18.3
Corporate	(13.6)	(7.5)	(66.6)	(17.3)	6.6	14.7
Continuing businesses	259.8	235.7	1,710.4	1,932.3	234.0	235.5
Discontinued businesses	(0.7)	5.6	27.7	76.3	2.9	6.0
	259.1	241.3	1,738.1	2,008.6	236.9	241.5

[1] Turnover and operating profit included in Europe relating to the UK amounted to £407.7 million (1985 £382.7 million) and £56.6 million (1985 £62.2 million) respectively.
[2] The US turnover and operating profit included in Americas were £963.6 million (1985 £986.5 million) and £104.0 million (1985 £106.2 million) respectively.

geographical segment data. Most UK companies provide such information separately rather than in a matrix form of presentation which would provide information on the interrelationship of the two types of segments (see Table 6.5). This presents another problem to the users of this information. Risk and expected return are both dependent upon the extent to which specific industry activities are committed to specific countries. A matrix presentation would mean that a more accurate assessment of company prospects would be possible. This is because the effect of changes in political, economic or social conditions in any country is dependent upon the specific industries that a company operates in.

6.5 The Benefits of Segmental Reporting

The possible benefits of segmental data have been examined using a variety of research techniques. Many of the earliest attempts simply asked users whether they required such information (e.g. Mautz, 1968; Backer and McFarland, 1968). However, whilst this approach may provide some valuable insights, it also suffers from several major problems or limitations. Of particular importance are the problems of ignorance and 'gaming'. If information is not currently provided or is provided by only a few companies, people may inaccurately assess either the value they would derive from such information or the problems and limitations inherent in its use. Gaming can occur if the users of accounts perceive the information contained in them to be costless or a free good. If this is the case then it is in their best interests to overstate the value of any information in an attempt to persuade companies to provide such information. Because of these problems, more direct tests of usefulness are necessary. Such tests are of two types: predictive ability (or forecasting) tests and stock market reaction tests.

Predictive ability tests compare the accuracy of forecasts of future sales or earnings based upon consolidated data to that of forecasts based on disaggregated data. Since future earnings are one of the main variables that investors are interested in, it is assumed that useful information is any information that helps to predict earnings. However, such an approach implicitly assumes that at least some shareholders are not only capable of using, but also will use, the information provided in this way. Whether or not this is the case is far from clear. Thus, the implications drawn from these indirect tests of usefulness have to be treated with some caution. The alternative approach, that of stock market reaction testing, appears to have somewhat greater validity. The idea is that if information has an effect upon the stock market then that information must have been used and so the usefulness of the data is tested directly. If the information has no effect, it is either irrelevant or has already been obtained from other sources so that there is no need for disclosure.

Predictive Ability

The first attempt to use segmental information for forecasting was by Kinney (1971), who forecast earnings for 24 companies for 1968 and 1969. The four models used are as follows:

Model 1	Consolidated earnings adjusted for forecast change in GNP
Model 2	Linear trend of earnings by double exponential smoothing with a smoothing constant of 0.4
Model 3	Expected segment sales × 3-year average consolidated profits ratio — where expected segment sales = current years sales × expected increase in industry sales
Model 4	Expected segment sales × 3-year average segment profit ratio. Segment sales as in Model 3.

Kinney found that Model 4 was significantly better than Models 1 and 2, and better (but not significantly) than Model 3. However, this study was very much an exploratory one and suffered from several major problems. In particular, not only was the sample very small but it only consisted of companies that voluntarily disclosed LOB data, so that self-selection bias may have existed; that is, there may have been features unique to these companies that meant that the conclusions were not applicable to the large group of non-disclosing companies. In addition, the choice of consolidated models appears to have been largely arbitrary rather than based upon research into the time series properties of earnings, so that the most accurate consolidated forecasting methods were probably not used. Indeed, no justification was provided for the choice of time series model made.

Collins (1976) remedied many of these limitations. The problems of self-selection bias and small sample size were avoided by using a random sample of 96 companies that reported after mandatory requirements were introduced. In addition, the consolidated models used were supported by the then existing time series literature. Actual sales and profits and first differences of each were forecast for 1968 to 1970 using the following models:

Consolidated models
1. Linear regression
2. Strict martingale or random walk
3. Submartingale or random walk with drift
4. Pure mean reversion
5. Moving average of pure mean reversion
6. Kinney's double exponential smoothing model
7. Kinney's GNP model

Segment models
Sales: based upon expected industry sales of each segment.
Earnings:
1. Expected segment sales × prior year consolidated profit margin.
2. Expected segment sales × prior year segment profit margin.

For actual sales it was found that the segment model significantly out-performed all the consolidated models, with the exception of the GNP model. For first differences the segment model out-performed all consolidated models except Model 1. For both the level and first differences of earnings the segmental models were significantly better than all the consolidated models, although the addition of segment profit margins only led to a marginal improvement in predictive ability over that achieved by segment sales and consolidated profit margin.

Silhan (1983) extended this analysis to examine the effects of quarterly information. This was done by creating multi-segment companies by merging 60 single-industry companies and applying company-specific or Box-Jenkins models to consolidated earnings, consolidated sales × consolidated margin, segment sales × consolidated margin, segment sales × segment margin and segment earnings. The advantage of this approach is that it allows the use of a very wide range of consolidated models as well as applying the most appropriate model to each company rather than one model to all the companies. He found that the conclusions of Kinney and Collins still held for both annual and one-quarter-ahead forecasts. All of these studies used US companies.

In a study using UK companies, Emmanuel and Pick (1980) forecast sales and earnings of 39 companies for the period 1973 to 1977. They found similar results in that segment-based turnover and earnings forecasts were more accurate than the random walk model. But they also found that the addition of segmental profit did not even lead to a marginal improvement over forecasts based upon segment sales and a consolidated profit margin.

One problem with all of these studies is that they ignored many company-specific factors. In particular, they ignored the number of segments reported and the size of company. Barefield and Comiskey (1975) examined the accuracy of Standard and Poor's earnings forecasts and found that the accuracy was significantly related to the amount of voluntary information disclosed. However, this relationship was significantly reduced once the number of segments was controlled. Silhan (1982), using simulated multi-segment companies, found some evidence that the forecasts were more accurate for those companies with the largest number of segments. Using the same methodology, Silhan (1984) found that the gain in predictive power due to the addition of segment data was more common for smaller companies, and that only for these companies were segment-based forecasts more accurate irrespective of the number of segments disclosed. He argued that this was probably because smaller segments are less likely to mirror the growth pattern of the overall economy or each other.

All of these studies reported above examined the behaviour of mechanical forecasts. An alternative approach is to examine the actual forecasts made by users. Baldwin (1984) examined the impact of financial analysts' forecasts of EPS reported by Value Line in 1969 to 1973. He examined forecasts of companies that voluntarily reported segment data prior to the introduction of SEC requirements, those that had not voluntarily disclosed segment data and a control group of single-segment companies. He found that accuracy improved and variability decreased over the period for all three groups (a result he was unable to explain) but that the greatest improvement occurred for the non-disclosure group. These results, again, support the conclusion that LOB disclosures lead to improved forecasts of earnings.

Stock Market Effects

Studies of the stock market effects of segmental information are mainly of two types: the market reaction to such disclosures and assessment of whether or not knowledge of segmental information would have led to better investment decisions. Kochanek (1974) classified 37 companies according to good and poor disclosers, and examined the correlation of past changes in share prices with current changes in earnings per share. He found a higher correlation for the companies with good disclosure but found only limited evidence of a decrease in variability of share prices. This is only an indirect test of stock market reactions. Horwitz and Kolodny (1977) failed to find any market reactions to the 10-K requirements for LOB disclosures. Simonds and Collins (1978) replicated this study, except that they classified the sample companies according to whether they had or had not voluntarily disclosed information prior to the 10-K requirements, and they used ANOVA rather than the F-test to test for changes in beta (the sensitivity of a share's price to changes in the price of shares generally). They found that disclosure of LOB data had the effect of significantly reducing beta. They also found very similar results with a moving beta test (Collins and Simonds, 1979). However, Ajinkya (1981) casts doubts upon these results. Specifically, he split the sample into sub-samples with high, medium and low betas during the initial estimation period, a mid-point period and a post-requirement period before carrying out the procedures employed by Simonds and Collins. Although he found a significant downward shift in beta for the two treatment groups he also found a similar shift for the multi-segment control group plus a tendency for high initial betas in the control groups to show mean reversion tendencies.

Rather than examining the effects on beta of segmental disclosures, an alternative approach is to examine the relationship of beta to the specific segmental disclosures made. Such an approach was followed by Kinney (1972) who attempted to use segment disclosures to study the market assessment of company diversification. He argued that accounting risk is the covariability of segment returns, which can be proxied by the covariability of segment earnings. He found that beta and accounting risk were significantly correlated for geographical disclosures but not for other types of disclosures. Mohr (1983 and 1985) employed an improved methodology to examine a similar question. Specifically, she employed segmental information to estimate the relative investment of companies in each activity and used these weights to compute a weighted beta which was then regressed upon the equity beta for 56 companies. She found a highly significant positive linear relationship between the two measures, especially when industry involvement was measured using asset data.

The other main approach used involves comparing the returns contingent upon an investment strategy based solely upon consolidated data and one based upon segmental data. The first of these studies was by Collins (1975). His sample consisted of 92 companies, examined for the effects of the introduction of the 10-K requirements, which meant that companies had to disclose prior year segmental information. Of these companies, 35 had disclosed no information prior to this, and the rest had disclosed segmented turnover. The strategy consisted of buying shares if the segment-based forecast earnings exceeded those from the consolidated models, and selling short if the reverse held. He found that the segment-based strategy failed to yield abnormal returns taking the period 1968 to 1970 as a whole. However, if 1970 was removed and only 1968 and 1969 considered, then the strategy yielded significant gains of between 1.44 and 1.51 per cent per month for companies that had disclosed no segmental information, but insignificant gains for those that had disclosed segmented turnover information prior to the 10-K requirements. Similar results were found by Foster (1977) who used a sample of insurance companies which reported underwriting results, investment results and losses on marketable securities for the period 1965–1972.

Ajinkya (1980) examined the average monthly risk-equalised returns of portfolios of companies that disclosed no information prior to the 10-K, those disclosing revenue only, those disclosing revenue and earnings, and single-segment companies. He found a greater correlation between the mean returns of the portfolios for the post-disclosure period. However, he failed to find any differences in the level of mean returns between the two periods. These findings are consistent with those of Dhaliwal (1978) who employed multiple regression techniques to examine changes in a return variance measure and a return dispersion measure following the SEC requirements. He also found evidence of a reduction in dispersion, which again implies increased consensus amongst market participants following the compulsory disclosure of line of business information.

The only study of geographical segment information has been by Prodhan (1986), using a sample of UK companies. These were 15 companies that had disclosed geographical data from at least 1973, and 21 that began to disclose such information in December 1977. Using interrupted time series analysis, he found that changes in beta were significantly related to segmental disclosures. Specifically, the treatment companies' betas were significantly higher than the control group's prior to disclosure, but not afterwards. In addition, the onset of the change was found to be abrupt rather than gradual.

Summary

Studies concerned with the prediction of earnings have all concluded that forecasts are more accurate if they are based upon segmented LOB turnover rather than on consolidated earnings. Those studies using US data have also found that forecasts based upon segment earnings are more accurate than forecasts based upon segment turnover. This has not been the case using UK data. In addition, there is some evidence that the relative accuracy of segment-based forecasts may depend upon the size of the company, with such disclosures being more useful for smaller companies.

There is evidence that disclosure of both LOB and geographical segment data result in a decrease in the market beta of the disclosing company. However, some of this evidence is inconclusive, with conflicting studies suggesting that such a relationship does not hold. Accounting-based betas formed from both geographical disclosures and LOB asset data appear to be correlated to market betas. However, LOB disclosures appear not to have affected the average risk-equalised returns of the disclosing companies, although there is some evidence that they have resulted in a decrease in the dispersion of market returns.

6.6 The Costs of Segmental Reporting

Several arguments against segmental disclosures have been propounded; some apply to all companies, others only in certain situations. It has been argued that the cost of compiling, processing and disseminating such information will exceed the benefits. However, to date there is no evidence available regarding the costs of disclosure, nor, indeed, any quantification of the benefits. In any event, this argument appears to have doubtful validity in most cases. Companies need disaggregated information for internal control and planning purposes and so produce some such information already. Even if the information used internally is not in a form suitable for external reporting, it seems unlikely, given the extensive use of computerised information systems, that the generation of such information will be particularly expensive. This is especially the case when it is realised just how much discretion companies have in deciding what constitutes a reportable segment. This means that, to a large extent, segments can be identified in such a way as to suit the already existing internal information systems.

Another and probably potentially more serious cost is that of dissemination of information which is of benefit to existing or potential competitors. This argument of competitive disadvantage appears to be very often used by companies to press for less restrictive information disclosure requirements (Gray and Roberts, 1988). While this may apply at the company level, especially if the same requirements do not apply to companies of other nationalities, it may not be a problem at the level of the economy as a whole. If such information aids competition then it might be considered as advantageous rather than as a cost to society. Whether or not this is the case will depend upon attitudes regarding the desirability of aiding competition as well as being largely case-specific, depending upon the characteristics of the industries and companies involved. However, it does appear that such information may be advantageous when seen in the wider societal perspective.

Another argument against the competitive disadvantage reason for non-disclosure is that such disclosures are only an attempt, and by no means a very successful one, at tipping the balance back in favour of single industry or country companies which disclose far more information about their single segment than do any multi-segment companies.

Probably the major argument against segmental information is that in some cases it may be inappropriate and so potentially misleading. The disclosure of segmental information implicitly assumes that the segments reported are relatively autonomous and independent of each other. This means that the figures reported for any one segment can be assessed independently from a consideration of the performance of the rest of the company. If, instead, the company is highly integrated, not only are there likely to be relatively large transfers between the segments, but also the segment results cannot be understood or considered in isolation from the rest of the company. At the extreme, if the company is very integrated, any disaggregated results are so arbitrary as to become meaningless. Unfortunately there is no evidence available regarding either the extent to which most companies are integrated nor what level of interdependence between parts of the company would invalidate segmental information. Thus, although this appears to be a significant problem for some companies, it is impossible to gauge its incidence in practice.

6.7 Conclusion

The growth of large diversified companies has presented problems for the users of accounts, especially in terms of assessing the future cash flows of a company and the risk or uncertainty associated with those future cash flows. Segmental reporting, or the disclosure of disaggregated data, is likely to go some way towards meeting the information needs of investors and other users.

While regulation is growing, and in the USA it is by far the most extensive, there remains the major problem of segment identification. The scope for managerial discretion provides substantial potential for the provision of misleading information. At the same time, it is noteworthy that the introduction of detailed rules may have had the effect of actually reducing the amount of information disclosed. There would seem to be scope, therefore, for guidelines which encourage disclosures and yet control their quality so that they are truly informative. In particular, the potential for more matrix presentations is clear, in that they seem likely to facilitate a more accurate assessment of company prospects.

The results of studies of predictive ability have shown that LOB segmental data are more useful than consolidated data for the prediction of earnings. While US results indicate that forecasts using segment earnings are more accurate than those using segment turnover, this has not been the case using UK data. There is also some evidence that the accuracy of forecasts is likely to be greater for small companies. As regards risk assessment, there is evidence to suggest that disclosure of both LOB and geographical segment data results in a decrease in market beta.

Potential constraints on the disclosure of segmental data include the costs of compiling, processing and disseminating information and, more significantly, the costs of competitive disadvantage. While companies often use the competitive disadvantage argument to counter attempts at further regulation or to justify non-disclosures, there may be a wider societal benefit from segmental reporting. Probably the major argument against such disclosure is that in some cases, where the company is highly integrated, it may be inappropriate and so potentially misleading.

References

AARF (1984) *Statement of Accounting Standards AAS 16, Financial Reporting by Segments*, issued by Australian Society of Accountants and Institute of Chartered Accountants of Australia.

ASC (1975) *The Corporate Report*, Accounting Standards Committee.

Ajinkya, B.B. (1980) 'An empirical evaluation of line of business reporting', *Journal of Accounting Research*, Autumn.

Ajinkya, B.B. (1981) 'Line of business reporting and market risk assessment: a methodological caveat', *Proceedings of the Southeast Regional Meeting, American Accounting Association*, May.
Arnold, J., Holder, W.W. and Mann, M.H. (1980) 'International reporting aspects of segment disclosure', *International Journal of Accounting*, Fall.
Backer, M. and McFarland, W.B. (1968) *External Reporting for Segments of a Business*, National Association of Accountants.
Baldwin, B.A. (1984) 'Segment earnings disclosure and the ability of security analysts to forecast earnings per share', *Accounting Review*, July.
Barefield, R. and Comiskey, E. (1975) 'Segmental financial disclosure by diversified firms and security prices: a comment', *Accounting Review*, October.
Buckley, J.W., Buckley, M.H. and Plank, T.M. (1980) *SEC Accounting*, Wiley.
CBI (1963) *The Responsibilities of the British Public Company*, Confederation of Business Industry.
CICA (1979) *Accounting Recommendations: General Accounting, Section 1700*, Canadian Institute of Chartered Accountants.
Collins, D.W. (1975) 'SEC product line reporting and market efficiency', *Journal of Financial Economics*, June.
Collins, D.W. (1976) 'Predicting earnings with sub-entity data: some further evidence', *Journal of Accounting Research*, Spring.
Collins, D.W. and Simonds, R. (1979) 'SEC line of business disclosure and market risk adjustments', *Journal of Accounting Research*, Autumn.
Dhaliwal, D. (1978) 'The impact of disclosure regulation on the cost of capital', in *Economic Consequences of Financial Accounting Standards, Selected Papers*, Financial Accounting Standards Board.
Emmanuel, C.R. and Gray, S.J. (1977) 'Segmental disclosures and the segment identification problem', *Accounting and Business Research*, Winter.
Emmanuel, C.R. and Pick, R. (1980) 'The predictive ability of UK segment reports', *Journal of Business Finance and Accounting*, Summer.
FASB (1976) *SFAS 14: Financial Reporting for Segments of a Business Enterprise*, Financial Accounting Standards Board.
Foster, G. (1977) 'Quarterly accounting data. Time series properties and predictive ability results', *Accounting Review*, January.
Gray, S.J. and Radebaugh, L.H. (1984) 'International segment disclosures by US and UK multinational enterprises: a descriptive study', *Journal of Accounting Research*, Spring.
Gray, S.J. and Roberts, C.B. (1988) 'Voluntary information disclosures and the British multinationals' in A.G. Hopwood (ed.), *International Pressures for Accounting Change*, Prentice-Hall.
HMSO (1962) *Report of the Company Law Committee*, Cmnd 1949.
HMSO (1977a) *The Future of Company Reports*, Cmnd 6888.
HMSO (1977b) *Report of the Committee of Inquiry into Industrial Democracy*, Cmnd 6706.
Horwitz, B. and Kolodny, R. (1977) 'Line of business reporting and security prices. An analysis of an SEC disclosure rule', *Bell Journal of Economics*, Spring.
IASC (1981) *IAS 14 Reporting Financial Information by Segments*, International Accounting Standards Committee.
ICAEW (1986) *Financial Reporting 1985–86*, Institute of Chartered Accountants in England and Wales.
Kinney, W.R. (1971) 'Predicting earnings: entity versus subentity data', *Journal of Accounting Research*, Spring.
Kinney, W.R. (1972) 'Covariability of segment earnings and multi-segment company returns', *Accounting Review*, April.

Kochanek, R.F. (1974) 'Segmental financial disclosures by diversified firms and security prices', *Accounting Review*, April.
Mautz, R.K. (1968) *Financial Reporting by Diversified Companies*, Financial Executives Research Foundation.
Mohr, R.M. (1983) 'The segment reporting issue; a review of empirical research', *Journal of Accounting Research*, Spring.
Mohr, R.M. (1985) 'The operating beta of a US multi-activity firm: an empirical investigation', *Journal of Business Finance and Accounting*, Winter.
OECD (1976) *International Investment and Multinational Enterprises*, OECD.
OECD (1979) *International Investment and Multinational Enterprises, Review of the 1976 Declaration Decisions*, OECD.
Oldham, K.M. (1987) *Accounting Systems and Practice in Europe*, Gower.
Prodhan, B.K. (1986) 'Geographical segment disclosures and multinational risk profile', *Journal of Business Finance and Accounting*, Spring.
Silhan, P.A. (1982) 'Simulated mergers of existent autonomous firms; a new approach to segmentation research', *Journal of Accounting Research*, Spring.
Silhan, P.A. (1983) 'The effects of segmenting quarterly sales and margins on extrapolative forecasts of conglomerate earnings: extension and replication', *Journal of Accounting Research*, Spring.
Silhan, P.A. (1984) 'Company size and the issue of quarterly segment reporting', *Journal of Accounting and Public Policy*, Fall.
Simonds, R. and Collins, D. (1978) 'Line of business reporting and security prices: an analysis of an SEC disclosure rule: a comment', *Bell Journal of Economics*, Autumn.
Stopford, J.M. (1983) *The World Directory of Multinational Enterprises 1982–83*, Macmillan.
Stopford, J.M. and Dunning, J.H. (1983) *Multinationals: Company Performance and Global Trends*, Macmillan.
United Nations (1977) *International Standards of Accounting and Reporting for Transnational Corporations*, UN Commission on Transnational Corporations.
United Nations (1982) *International Standards of Accounting and Reporting*, Report of the Ad Hoc Intergovernmental Working Group of Experts on International Standards of Accounting and Reporting, UN Commission on Transnational Corporations.

7

International Financial Analysis

STUART J. McLEAY

7.1 Introduction

This chapter is concerned with the analysis of financial statements in an international setting. One important application is the analysis of the operations of a multinational company, where the financial statements result from a process of aggregation of underlying transactions which have been carried out in a number of countries and denominated in various currencies. Another dimension of international financial analysis is cross-national comparison between companies which are based in different countries but which do not necessarily have multinational activities. Finally, and regardless of the nature of the company or companies under scrutiny, our concern could be with the geographical spread not of companies but of the users of corporate reports, where the analysis is carried out by residents of different countries — Italian investors, American bankers, or Japanese fund managers, for instance — with their own particular expectations about corporate activity.

Whilst each of these distinctive 'international' dimensions of financial statement analysis is important, the basic process of financial communication remains the same. Essentially, we are concerned in each case with financial information which has crossed national boundaries at some stage or other. Of course, in so doing, financial statistics may be restated and financial terminology may be translated. For instance, some of the

Acknowledgement
The author is grateful to Susan Fieldsend for research assistance funded by ESRC under the 'Statistical Modelling of Corporate Financial Indicators' project. Also, Section 7.4 is based on joint research into transnational financial reporting carried out with Simon Archer, the preliminary results of which have been published elsewhere (see Archer and McLeay, 1987).

information disclosed by a multinational has already been restated and translated during the consolidation of group accounts. On the other hand, in the case of a cross-national comparison, it is the analyst who has to confront the problems of restating financial statistics and translating financial terminology. Thus, some of the key issues in international financial analysis are concerned with the restatement and translation of financial reports which describe operations conducted in one environment but which are the subject of review and analysis in another.

Accordingly, in this chapter, we shall consider ways in which a company's financial disclosures may be influenced by its operating environment, how companies report on these issues and, finally, how analysts deal with the issues that are raised.

7.2 The Usefulness of Financial Statement Information

It has been suggested that the information in financial statements has been digested by the market makers before the accounts are publicly available. Therefore, a basic issue is whether or not the analysis of financial statement information is a worthwhile undertaking (see Foster, 1986, for a review). But others such as Arnold & Moizer (1984) and Day (1986) suggest that financial statement information is useful, at least in the eyes of analysts in the United Kingdom, and there have been similar studies leading to similar

Table 7.1 Financial Analysts' Ranking of Corporate Annual Report Parts, In Order of Relative Importance

	USA	*UK*	*NZ*
Income statement	1	1	1
Summary of operations for the last 5–10 years	7	10	3
Balance sheet	2	1	2
Statement of changes in financial position	3	3	4
Sales and income by product line	5	4	7
Management's discussion and analysis of the summary of operations	9	5	5
Other footnotes	6	7	8
Accounting policies	4	6	9
Auditor's report	10	9	10
Form 10-K report	8	11	11
President's letter	11	8	6
Pictorial material	12	12	12

conclusions in other countries. There is one research study which addresses this issue on an international scale (Chang, Most & Brain, 1983), where the utility of annual reports to individual investors, institutional investors and financial analysts is compared across three countries: the USA, the UK and New Zealand. It was found that financial statements are perceived as the most important information source among a variety of potential sources on which investment decisions may be based. But, more interestingly, Chang, Most and Brain found inter-country differences in the importance attached to some parts of the corporate annual report, as shown in Table 7.1.

Perhaps these inter-country differences in the perceived importance of annual report disclosures are merely a reflection of the fact that the conventions of financial reporting differ from country to country. For instance, it is not very surprising that New Zealand investors show little interest in the Form 10-K report! But perhaps the lesson is this: balance sheets, income statements and funds statements are relatively common, and there is widespread availability of accounting data. The problems of inter-firm comparability are as much a domestic issue as one that is central to international financial analysis. Indeed, whilst accounting method differs from country to country, it also varies considerably from company to company, due in part to the very real differences in company operations. In the latter context, supplementary information about a company's policies is crucial. Similarly, in international financial analysis, the analyst needs information about local operating environments and the local laws and customs which influence the financial accounts.

When commenting on international comparisons of financial ratios, Foster (1986) suggests that it is important to consider a number of factors before making inferences based on observed differences in the financial ratios of companies. These are:

1. differences in the set of accounting principles adopted in each country;
2. differences in taxation rules adopted in each country and in the relationship between the accounting principles used for tax and those used for financial reporting;
3. differences in the financing, operation, and other business arrangements in each country;
4. differences in the cultural, institutional, and the political environment in each country.

In effect, the analyst needs to be able to account for these institutional and cultural factors, in order to determine the 'residual' behaviour that is attributable to (say) a given company's operating capacity. But these country effects are pervasive, and indeed there is considerable interaction between the company's performance or structure and its immediate operating environment. In the next section, we focus on some of these complex issues.

7.3 Understanding Differences in Accounting Method

It is not necessary here to provide evidence that inter-country differences in accounting method exist; there is a substantial literature on this subject (see Chapters 2 and 3, for example). However, in an international context, it is important to understand why country-to-country differences in accounting method persist, and whether they merely reflect divergence of opinion on an aspect of accounting policy over which there is a choice, or whether they reveal deeper structural differences attributable to the legal and social system and to the financial environment in a given country. Below, are a number of illustrations of this point.

Different Social Systems

Table 7.2 shows how the accounting treatment of supplementary employee remuneration influences the computation of funds generated from operations for three companies (one British, one Italian and one French). We start in column one with the British company which places all pension provisions with a financial institution and, in this case of course, the 'funds' in question leave the company. For a company operating in France, there is a statutory requirement that part of the company's profits be allocated for the benefit of employees, with reinvestment in external assets within two years. In the short-term, we could consider that there is an element in Funds Generated from Operations (+F. 800 in the example) which relates

Table 7.2 The Impact of Different Remuneration Schemes on Funds Generated from Operations

	UK	*France*	*Italy*
	(£)	(*Francs*)	(*Lire*)
Earnings	100	1,000	100,000
Add back:			
Depreciation of fixed assets	250	2,500	250,000
Provision for employee pensions	80	—	—
less: funds applied in the current year	(80)	—	—
Share of profits attributable to employees	—	800	—
less: funds applied in the current year	—	(700)	—
Deferred employee remuneration	—	—	80,000
less: funds applied in the current year	—	—	(30,000)
Funds generated from operations	350	3,600	400,000

to the allocation for the current period, whilst the only outflow is the cash placed in external investments (−F. 700).

Now compare these two approaches with the situation in Italy, where employees are entitled on leaving a company to one month's salary (at current rates of pay) for each year in service. There is no requirement for the company to place these funds in earmarked investments, although the appropriate provisions must be made. Thus, Funds Generated from Operations includes the provision (+L. 80,000) net of the payment to retiring employees (−L. 30,000).

Of course, there are many ways of constructing a Funds Statement, and the example is not uncontentious. However, it shows that the issues of accounting method and social structure are not unrelated. Indeed, we are drawn into a debate about the nature of the entity – what sort of funds are these, and what are the broader implications of providing for employee shares in profit and deferred employee remuneration? We might easily imagine an Italian company whose net assets are funded not only by (i) shareholder's equity and (ii) interest-bearing debt, but also by (iii) an additional substantial stake neither bearing interest nor sharing in profits but nevertheless with an accumulator based on wage inflation. It certainly throws the simple notion of gearing into some confusion. And the confusion arises because the simplistic model of a company financed by debt and equity no longer seems to fit the social circumstances.

Clearly, the example shows that when we compare the funds generated by companies in different countries, part of the explanation of the variability in levels of self-financing lies in the different social systems within which the companies operate.

Different Financial Systems

In spite of the moves in the European Community to bring about an integrated financial system, there exist aspects of corporate financing which are idiosyncratic. For example, it is commonplace in many European countries for the extension of trade credit to be supported by a discountable bill, where a company may either allow a trade debt to run to maturity or alternatively discount the bill receivable. In the latter circumstances, whilst the company's liquid funds will increase, a contingent liability to the discounting bank exists until the debt has been realised. For example, a trade debt of 1,000 Francs could appear in any one of the following balance sheet lines:

Accounts receivable	F. 1,000
or:	
Bills receivable	F. 1,000
or:	
Cash at bank	F. 975

where, in the latter case, it is assumed that the discount is 25 Francs. One interpretation is that discounting effectively restates trade debt at current values, rather than being stated at the amounts collectable at some future date (although the difference is likely to be relatively trivial). Of more importance is the effect on the measurement of liquid funds, and it could be argued that bills receivable, which are immediately realisable, should be included.

Clearly, the 'liquidity' of a company depends to some extent on the mechanisms that exist within a financial system to provide liquidity, and bill discounting is one such mechanism that is commonplace in some European countries and not in others. Hence, we can conclude that differences in liquid funds are in part explained by the nature of the financial systems in which companies operate.

An interesting study of international differences in liquidity, gearing and other aspects of corporate structure has been carried out by Choi and others (1983). They compared financial ratios of US companies with those of Japanese and Korean firms, using aggregate statistics for large samples of manufacturing companies in each country. Some of the differences are substantial, as shown in Table 7.3.

Table 7.3 Differences in Liquidity and Gearing

	USA (976 firms)	*Japan (354 firms)*	*Korea (902 firms)*
Current ratio	1.94	1.15	1.13
Total debt to total assets	0.47	0.84	0.78
Times interest earned	6.50	1.60	1.80

Japanese and Korean firms appear less liquid and more highly geared than their US counterparts. But is this a result of differences in accounting practice or is it due to structural differences in corporate financing? In fact, for a matched sample of companies from the three countries, the authors restated the financial ratios using accounting principles generally accepted in the US and found that the accounting restatements have little effect on the intercountry differences in liquidity and gearing (and a number of other aspects of corporate structure and performance). The main factors explaining differences in corporate liquidity and gearing appear to be 'country effects', such as (i) the strong interdependence between banks and corporate firms in Japan and Korea where debt assumes many of the characteristics of preferred stock, and (ii) the open market for corporate debt in the USA (including the 'junk bond' market) which explains to some extent why companies in that country have less short-term exposure, and hence lower ratios of current assets to current liabilities.

In this case, then, we find that the nature of the financial systems within which companies operate contributes to explaining variability in corporate financial indicators.

Differences in the Conventions of Accounting

It is usual to distinguish between short-term debt and long-term debt in a company balance sheet, and no doubt somewhere in the annals of accounting history there will be an explanation as to why it is conventional to assume that debt repayable in less than one year is 'short-term'. But, as it happens, that convention is not universal. For example, let us consider the following debt contracts and draw up a Balance Sheet at 31–12–1986:

1. Debt contract dated 30–6–79,	maturity 30–6–87	50,000
2. Debt contract dated 1–7–86,	maturity 1–7–94	200,000
3. Debt contract dated 1–7–86,	maturity 1–7–89	75,000

First, we present the financial statements that would be presented by a company operating in the UK.

British company: balance sheet at 31st December 1986	
Long-term debt	275,000
Short-term debt	50,000

In contrast, a company operating in West Germany subdivides its debt on a quite different basis, and amongst long-term liabilities will be those debt contracts of over four years, whilst shorter-term debt will include those contracts whose original maturity was under four years.[1] The length of time to maturity at the balance sheet date is not taken into account and, although certain companies will disclose supplementary information allowing a restatement in accordance with the more common definition of short-term, the standard German presentation would be as follows:

West German company: balance sheet at 31st December 1986	
Long-term debt (contract > 4 years)	250,000
Short-term debt (contract < 4 years)	75,000

The conclusion is this. Differences in the financial structure of companies, as presented in their financial statements, must be explained by

[1] Note that the provisions of the 1985 German Act should bring about a change in this practice from 1987 year-end onwards.

a number of factors, including (i) those which result from the constraints of the domestic financial system, (ii) those which are merely a peculiarity of accounting method, and finally (iii) a residual element attributable to the financial policies adopted by the company in question.

The Influence of the State

Let us consider here the situation in Sweden. A particular feature of Swedish accounting is the Investment Reserve. Companies may allocate up to 50 per cent of income before taxes to the investment reserves, and in some years the government may require allocations to these reserves. For example, in 1984 companies were required to allocate 20 per cent of income before taxes to a special investment reserve. An additional requirement is that companies must deposit funds equal to a portion of the allocations in a non-interest-bearing account with the Bank of Sweden. The proportion of the allocation to be deposited varies from year to year, but at the present time companies must make a deposit equal to 75 per cent of last year's allocations. These funds may be withdrawn from the Bank of Sweden when approved investments are made in property, plant and equipment, where approval is given by the Swedish government or the National Industrial Board following a process of consultation with the appropriate employee organisations.

The fiscal implications are substantial. Swedish companies are able to reduce tax payments by making tax-deductible allocations to untaxed reserves, such as the Investment Reserve described above. The allocations are recognised in determining Net Income for the year, and corresponding credits are made to Untaxed Reserves in the balance sheet. The effect of these discretionary allocations is considerable: for instance, with a corporate tax rate of 52 per cent, the Swedish car and truck manufacturer Volvo has been able to reduce its effective tax rate to between 20 per cent and 30 per cent in recent years. Of course, allocations can be reversed but the reduction becomes subject to tax. In fact, reversal of prior allocations is usually adopted to avoid reporting a loss, in which circumstances it does not result in a corresponding tax payment.

In addition to the allocations to the Investment Reserve, other discretionary allocations may be based upon inventories and payrolls. At present, inventory reserves cannot exceed 50 per cent of year-end reserves after deductions for obsolescence, and payroll reserves are limited to 20 per cent of annual wages and salaries. In spite of the limits imposed, these are still substantial fiscal incentives. As in certain other European countries, these fiscal allocations are accounted for explicitly in the income statement, rather than using some form of deferred taxation arrangement to bridge the gap. Clearly, the analyst who wishes to compare the earnings of a Swedish company with a foreign competitor will need to consider some kind of adjustment to the published figures.

The impact on financial structure is also important. Untaxed Reserves may be viewed as a combination of shareholders' equity and deferred taxation, where the latter is similar to interest-free debt for an indefinite period. Again, the conventional simplistic notions of leverage are thrown into some confusion by this alternative approach to company financing where the state acts as a major financial partner.

It is interesting to see how Volvo deals with these issues. The financial report (including the original Swedish version) contains a reconciliation between Net Income in accordance with Swedish accounting principles and Net Income in accordance with US GAAP. The treatment of allocations to untaxed reserves is as follows:

	1986 *Kr(m.)*
Net income in accordance with Swedish accounting principles	**2,551**
Add: Allocations to untaxed reserves	2,694
Less: Deferred income taxes	(1,547)
Other adjustments	(742)
Net income in accordance with US GAAP	**2,956**

For 1986, the effects of accounting differences on Net Income were not extreme. However, Volvo restates its equity along similar lines, and we can see that the effect on accumulated retentions is far more substantial:

	1986 *Kr(m.)*
Shareholders' equity in accordance with Swedish accounting principles	**10,124**
Add: Untaxed reserves	20,980
Less: Deferred income taxes	(11,950)
Other adjustments	938
Equity in accordance with US GAAP	**20,092**

For reference, the tangible assets were as follows:

Tangible assets	**71,589**

and it is clear that the effects of state policies with respect to Investment Reserves and other fiscal devices are considerable in the case of this company.

Other Influences: A Comparison Between France, West Germany and the UK

As we have already seen, the methods used in the calculation of company profits vary considerably from country to country, and it has been argued here that there are many factors which influence the calculation of accounting profits, including legal requirements, professional accounting standards, tax law, the structure and development of capital markets, and so on. But are we able to quantify these effects in some way? In an interesting comparative empirical study of profits reported by large companies in France, West Germany and the UK, Gray (1980) showed that there is a tendency for companies in certain countries to be relatively 'conservative' in profit measurement, and he gave some indication of the importance of this apparent bias. As a basis of comparison, Gray used the adjusted earnings figures computed and published by one of Europe's leading information intermediaries, DAFSA. An indicator of measurement behaviour, CI, was calculated by standardising the difference between adjusted earnings R_A and disclosed earnings R_D, such that $CI = 1 - (R_A - R_D)/|R_A|$ is equal to 1 when disclosed earnings and adjusted earnings are equal, and less than 1 when profits disclosure is relatively conservative (i.e. the amount disclosed is less than the earnings figure attributed to the company by the external analyst). Of course, the study relates to a particular period, but the results showed an intense conservatism in Germany and a similar tendency towards conservatism in France. Grouping the scores from an extensive analysis into three categories to represent what the author termed:

I. 'pessimistic' profit measurement, where CI is less than 0.95,
II. relatively neutral calculation, where $0.95 < CI < 1.05$, and
III. 'optimistic' reporting where CI is greater than 1.05,

Gray obtained the results which are set out in Table 7.4.

Table 7.4 A Comparative Analysis of Profit Measurement Behaviour (percentage of companies falling into classes I, II and III)

	France	*West Germany*	*UK*
I. Pessimistic ($CI < 0.95$)	77	75	14
II. Neutral ($0.95 < CI < 1.05$)	8	8	28
III. Optimistic ($CI > 1.05$)	15	17	58

One explanation that has been offered for these differences is the influence of tax law. But Gray also suggests that the orientation towards different groups of users is an important factor, with an emphasis in the UK on equity investors who are presumed to be primarily interested in profits available for distribution, whereas the orientation in France and West Germany is assumed to be towards creditors and debt financiers who are more likely to be concerned with the capacity of the company to fund its interest payments. Thus, in the study by Gray, it is concluded that the behaviour of company management is likely to be strongly influenced by user demands, and that 'generous measures of distributable profits would be contrary to (creditors') interests just as much as conservative profits would tend to be a disservice to the equity investor'. In fact, this view is held in many quarters. For instance, the following comment appeared recently in the *Financial Times* Lex column:

> The traditional p/e ratio comparison has been dogged not just by particular national discrepancies in, say, the consolidation of subsidiaries, but by entirely different philosophies of financial reporting. Simply put, US and UK accounts are directed primarily at current and potential investors and thus tend to provide a realistic estimate of earnings, while German and Japanese accounts are drawn up with the tax authorities in mind and therefore understate earnings.

This underlines the complexity of the issues with which we are concerned. Not only are there country effects as indicated earlier, and differences attributable to divergence of accounting method, there are also likely to be substantial interactions, where companies choose particular accounting policies because of the nature of the society within which they operate.

Conceptual Differences

A possibility that we have not considered yet is that economic concepts may vary, leading to different ways in which the underlying concept is operationalised in accounting terms. Value added is a good example in this context.

Value added, it is said, represents a firm's contribution to the wealth generated in an economy. According to some, it is identical to the corporate share in the National Product. But the definition of 'National Product' is open to debate. For instance, Quesnay, the French originator of the concept of national income who introduced the notion of intermediate consumption within an economy, was also in favour of deducting a replacement provision for the maintenance of fixed and working capital. Later, it was recognised that some intermediate consumption arises from durables (i.e. those which require time in order to be consumed) and Marxian labour value theory led to a definition of 'new value in output', added to durable and non-durable intermediates, i.e. Net Material Product. On the other hand, Gross Domestic Product has been defined as 'the sum of government and private final consumption expenditure, gross capital formation in fixed assets and stocks and exports minus imports of goods and services'. In this case, to use the accountants' term, 'depreciation' is not deducted. And, finally, there is the view that national product consists of the goods and services received during a given period by individuals in their capacity as consumers, which excludes those discounted values which will produce benefits to be consumed in future periods.

In other words, we have at our disposal many economic concepts of value added. The question is: do we find similar variety in the approaches to value added measurement that are adopted in different countries? Furthermore, are the differences in approach consistent with competing concepts? A study of the methods of value added computation adopted by British and German companies (McLeay, 1983) attempted to find out whether inter-country differences in value added measurement may be associated with alternative conceptual models.

In the first instance, let us consider an example based on the following stock flow:

	Cost of materials	*Cost of labour*	*Net income*	*Total*
Sales	53	57	40	150
Increase in stock	7	8	4	19
Production	60	65	44	169

Accordingly, we can derive the following simplified value-added statements:

	Net of unrealised revenues (UK method)	*Net of unrealised profits (West German method)*	*At selling prices*
Output	150	165	169
less: Materials	53	60	60
Value added	97	105	109
Attributable as follows:			
Employees	57	65	65
Company	40	40	44

The example above shows how British companies derive value added from trading (i.e. sales = 150), whilst West German companies take a production-oriented view (where output is stated at 165 which includes sales 150, plus the increase in stocks 19, net of unrealised profits 4).

In effect, West German companies use a concept of value added which includes that part of unrealised revenues that is attributable to employees, whilst British companies exclude all unrealised revenues from value added. In other words, as shown in the example, the difference between value added using the West German method (105) and value added using the UK method (97) is equal to the labour cost element in the increase in stock (8).

Another key difference in practice concerns the treatment of depreciation. West German companies deduct depreciation along with other intermediate consumption, whereas British companies do not. For instance, if we extend the previous example by assuming a depreciation charge of 10 and a profit figure of 25, the effect would be to reduce the value added disclosed by a West German company as follows:

	UK method	*West German method*
Output	150	165
less: Materials	53	60
Depreciation	–	15
Value added	97	90
Attributable as follows:		
Employees	57	65
Company	40	25

The question that remains is this: do these inter-country differences in value added measurement reflect conscious choices between alternative conceptual models? The evidence is not clear. In West Germany, it has been suggested that the choice of method is dictated by corporate positioning in bargaining with the employee group, as the value added statement is an instrument of public relations for use in this bargaining process. Another explanation is that the selection of a particular method is no more than an accident, related more to the dominant conventions of accounting than to the choice of a particular conceptual model. For instance, the differing orientations are also evident within income statements in the two countries: West German companies deriving profit from output in their legally-prescribed income statements, whilst the practice in the UK has generally been for companies to report the derivation of profit from sales. The EC's fourth Directive makes this choice explicit.

7.4 Disclosure Practices in International Financial Reporting

The examples given above demonstrate clearly that the analysis of financial statements in an international context requires information about:

(i) aspects of a company's domestic operating environment which exert an influence on its structure and performance;
(ii) accounting methods which are peculiar to the country in question.

Companies experiencing a demand for this information may respond by supplying it, sometimes because regulatory institutions mandate such disclosures (as is the case with the SEC's requirement that foreign companies whose shares are listed in the USA should file Form 20–F), and sometimes on a voluntary basis.

In fact, companies adopt various approaches to transnational financial disclosure, including:

(i) the use of notes explaining to the foreign reader the peculiarities of the domestic accounting principles used, perhaps with a glossary of the technical expressions used;
(ii) some kind of restatement of the financial results using an alternative set of accounting principles;
(iii) a restatement of the results in the currency used by the foreign reader;
(iv) a direct translation of their annual report into other languages, or publication of a condensed translated version for foreign users.

Notes and Glossaries for the Foreign Reader

Some of the larger international companies go to considerable lengths to inform their foreign report users of the particularities of the company's operating environment. Volkswagen, for instance, include a small lexicon within their report explaining (amongst many other things) their distinctive approach to value added measurement. Volvo include a separate Reader's Guide to the English language and French language editions of their annual report, along with illustrative examples of the intricacies of Swedish reserve accounting. Other companies include supplementary notes to the financial statements, which appear solely in foreign language versions of the annual report, and which tend usually to describe the domestic tax and accounting regulations.

Restatement of Results in Accordance with Internationally Recognised Accounting Principles

It would seem that the process of international standardisation of accounting principles should facilitate comparability between the financial statements of companies operating in different countries. At present, however, many companies, whose financial statements are drawn up in accordance with local regulations, attempt to assist their foreign report users by restating the accounts using internationally recognised accounting principles. For instance, the Finnish company Wartsila includes in its annual report summarised financial statements in accordance with International Accounting Standards, a practice now adopted by several Finnish companies. Wartsila explains this approach as follows:

> Considering the extensiveness of Wartsila's international operations and the fact that Wartsila shares, apart from Helsinki, are also listed on the

Table 7.5 The Use of International Accounting Standards by Wartsila

Adjustments to Income Statement	*1985*	*1984*
Profit for the financial year in accordance with IAS	**229**	723
Adjustments to change in inventories to include appropriate proportion of overhead expenses	**(61)**	6
Difference between historical cost depreciation and recorded depreciation	**(136)**	(111)
Other appropriations to inventory and other reserves	**209**	(411)
Share of profits in associated companies	**(40)**	(51)
Movement in provision of warranty costs	**5**	5
Profit for the financial year in accordance with Finnish law and practice	**206**	161

Adjustments to Shareholders' Equity	*1985*	*1984*
Shareholders' equity in accordance with IAS	**3,812**	3,671
Inclusion in inventories of appropriate proportion of production overhead expenses	**(389)**	(327)
The accumulative difference between recorded and historical cost depreciation	**(589)**	(453)
Reclassification of inventory and other reserves	**(1,297)**	(1,508)
Restatement of investments in associated companies at appropriate proportion of adjusted net assets	**(106)**	(66)
Provision of expected liabilities in connection with warranties to customers	**70**	65
Shareholders' equity in accordance with Finnish law and practice	**1,501**	1,382

Key Figures Based on IAS

		1981	*1982*	*1983*	*1984*	**1985**
Net sales	MFIM	3,058	3,864	5,419	6,243	**5,546**
Profit for the financial year before extraordinary items	MFIM	208	362	499	736	**454**
Earnings/share	FIM	31	53	63	80	**47**
Dividend/share	FIM	3.33	4.48	4.97	7.80	**7.80**
Net assets per share	FIM	250	277	323	377	**391**
Return on shareholders' equity	%	12	19	20	23	**6**
Debt to equity ratio		1.9	2.0	1.9	1.7	**1.7**

Stockholm and London Stock Exchanges, group financial statements are presented in a more familiar form for the international reader.

For example, the reconciliations in Table 7.5 appear in Wartsila's annual report, and the company draws attention to the earnings trends and to its gearing using the IAS results.

However, most international companies that provide restated figures adopt accounting principles that are generally accepted in the USA. Whilst certain stock exchanges, such as the International Stock Exchange in London, make some mention of international accounting standards in the context of disclosure requirements for listing by foreign companies, the major influence is the SEC which stipulates that foreign companies whose shares are traded in the US must file a set of financial statements prepared using US GAAP.

A point to note is that not all international companies include these supplementary restated figures in their annual report, even the annual report prepared for US investors! This is certainly an area where the analyst should seek the full set of disclosures made by a company.

Translation into Foreign Currencies

These are known as 'convenience currency translations' as the aim is primarily to re-express the financial results in another currency merely for the convenience of the reader. A good example is the multi-currency reporting format adopted by Unilever (see Table 7.6). This particular multinational is a special case, as the Dutch parent company and the UK parent company are linked by an equalisation agreement and combine their results to present consolidated figures for the group as a whole. Note, for instance, the presentation of earnings, dividends and equity per share in Table 7.6. Separate results are given for the 20 Florin shares issued by the Dutch parent and the 25 pence shares issued by the British parent. The translation effects can be significant. Compare, for example, the sales figures for 1985 and the 1984 corresponding figures:

	1985	*1984*	*% difference*
Dutch parent (in Dutch guilders)	Fl. 42,592	Fl. 40,790	−4.2
UK parent (in pounds sterling)	£ 5,859	£ 6,496	+10.9
Combined operations:			
in Dutch guilders	Fl. 66,791	Fl. 66,771	−0.03
in pounds sterling	£ 16,172	£ 16,693	+3.2
in US dollars	$ 18,760	$ 24,205	−4.2

In this case, the group's accounting policy is to consolidate subsidiaries

Table 7.6 Multicurrency Reporting by Unilever

1985 above 1984	*Sterling Pounds*	*Dutch Guilders*	*Austrian Schillings*	*Belgian Francs*	*French Francs*	*German Marks*	*Swiss Francs*	*US Dollars*
Rates of exchange £1=[a]		**4.00**	**24.95**	**72.60**	**10.90**	**3.55**	**2.99**	**1.45**
		4.13	25.67	73.23	11.20	3.66	3.01	1.16
	In millions of currency							
Turnover	**16,693**	**66,771**	**416,487**	**1,211,902**	**181,952**	**59,260**	**49,912**	**24,205**
	16,172	66,791	415,137	1,184,280	181,127	59,190	48,678	18,760
Operating profit	**949**	**3,797**	**23,683**	**68,912**	**10,346**	**3,370**	**2,838**	**1,376**
	930	3,841	23,875	68,110	10,417	3,404	2,800	1,078
Profit on ordinary activities before taxation	**953**	**3,814**	**23,788**	**69,219**	**10,392**	**3,385**	**2,851**	**1,382**
	925	3,823	23,765	67,795	10,369	3,388	2,787	1,073
Profit on ordinary activities after taxation	**556**	**2,223**	**13,863**	**40,340**	**6,056**	**1,973**	**1,661**	**805**
	537	2,218	13,787	39,332	6,015	1,966	1,617	622
Profit on ordinary activities attributable to shareholders	**516**	**2,064**	**12,876**	**37,467**	**5,625**	**1,832**	**1,543**	**748**
	503	2,078	12,918	36,851	5,636	1,842	1,515	583
Ordinary dividends	**179**	**718**	**4,482**	**13,042**	**1,958**	**638**	**537**	**260**
	165	684	4,248	12,120	1,854	606	498	192
Profit of the year retained	**333**	**1,330**	**8,296**	**24,139**	**3,624**	**1,180**	**994**	**482**
	308	1,270	7,899	22,535	3,447	1,126	926	357

In units of currency

Earnings per share								
Per Fl. 20 of capital	**919.71p**	**36.79**	**229.50**	**667.67**	**100.24**	**32.66**	**27.53**	**13.33**
	895.56p	37.01	230.00	656.15	100.37	32.78	27.01	10.39
Per 25p of capital	**137.96p**	**5.52**	**34.42**	**100.15**	**15.04**	**4.90**	**4.13**	**2.00**
	134.33p	5.55	34.50	98.42	15.06	4.92	4.05	1.56
Ordinary dividends [b]								
NV – per Fl. 20 of capital	**370.50p**	**14.82**	**92.45**	**268.97**	**40.38**	**13.16**	**11.09**	**5.37**
	341.65p	14.11	87.69	250.18	38.27	12.50	10.30	3.96
PLC – per 25p of capital	**38.62p**	**1.54**	**9.64**	**28.04**	**4.21**	**1.37**	**1.15**	**0.56**
	35.52p	1.47	9.12	26.01	3.98	1.30	1.07	0.41
Shareholders' equity per share								
Per Fl. 20 of capital	**5,949.40p**	**237.92**	**1,484.23**	**4,318.00**	**648.29**	**211.22**	**178.02**	**86.20**
	6,008.69p	248.14	1,542.18	4,399.59	673.00	219.80	181.12	69.70
Per 25p of capital	**892.41p**	**35.69**	**222.63**	**647.70**	**97.24**	**31.68**	**26.70**	**12.93**
	901.30p	37.22	231.33	659.94	100.95	32.97	27.17	10.46

Movements between 1984 and 1985 will vary according to the currencies in which the figures are expressed.

[a] Rates of exchange are respective year-end rates used in translating the combined figures in the various currencies.

[b] The value of dividends received by shareholders in currencies other than sterling or guilders will be affected by fluctuations in the rates of exchange after the year-end.

of the Dutch parent into guilders, and subsidiaries of the UK parent into pounds, using the exchange rates current at the respective year-ends for translation of income statement items and for assets and liabilities at the year-end. The effect of exchange rate changes during the year on the assets and liabilities at the beginning of the year is recorded as a movement in profit retained. The combined figures are also arrived at using year-end rates and, for the sales figures above, the following exchange rates applied at the end of 1985: £1 = Fl. 4.00 = $1.45 (1984: £1 = Fl. 4.13 = $1.16). The movement in the US dollar against the guilder and the pound sterling clearly has a substantial effect on the representation of Unilver's results in dollars.

As Unilever show, standard accounting practices in the area of currency translation can be applied to the problems of international financial reporting. But not many companies appear to do so, and such companies often make it clear that these foreign currency reports are presented 'solely

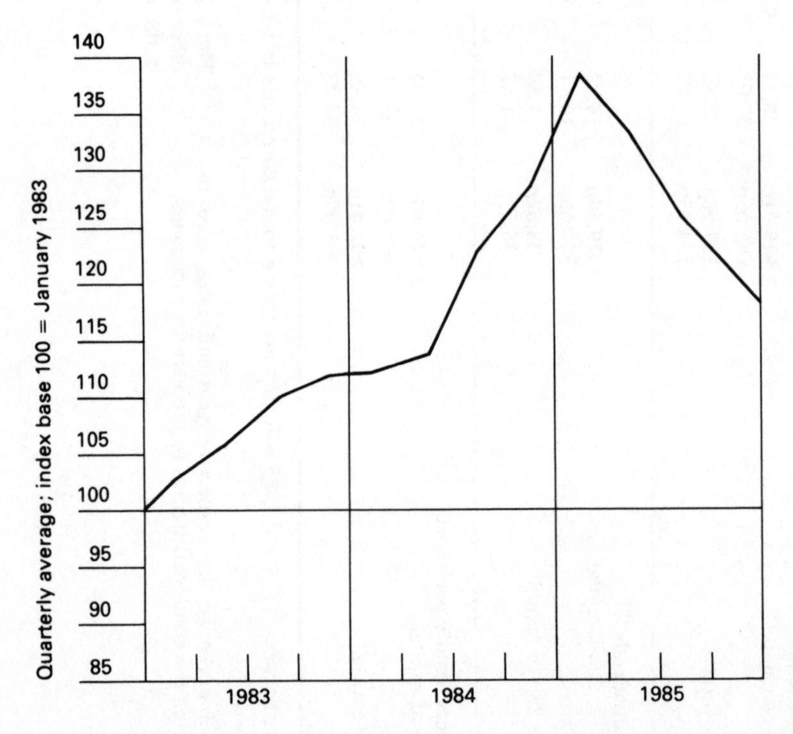

Note: The 'Shell currency basket' comprises the currencies of 14 major countries weighted by the sales proceeds of Group Companies outside North America.

Figure 7.1 Movement of US Dollar against Shell Currency Basket

for the pupose of convenience'. Indeed, the present regulations of the SEC do not permit translation into US dollars in the 20–F filing, but require the financial statements to be presented in their source currency. However, in their annual reports, we find that companies will use one of a number of different approaches in this unregulated area, such as:

(i) average rates for income statement items and year-end rates for assets and liabilities;
(ii) average rates for all amounts;
(iii) year-end rates for all amounts where, in some cases and unlike the example given above, the rate for the current year-end is applied not only to the current year's figures but also to the corresponding figures for the previous year.

One innovation that is worth mentioning is the use of composite currencies for reporting on the affairs of an international company to an international investment community. The French company, St Gobain, is known for pioneering the use of the ECU (the European Currency Unit) in this context, and there are other examples of currency cocktails, such as Interflora's aptly named Fleurin. Another good example appears in the annual report of Royal Dutch Shell, who use a currency basket comprising the currencies of major countries weighted by the sales proceeds of group companies denominated in those currencies. Whilst, in this latter case, the financial statements are not presented using a composite, the extract from the Royal Dutch report given in Figure 7.1 shows how the company's sales outside North America have moved against the dollar in recent years.

Linguistic Issues

It does seem that when a company reports to an international audience it will tend to translate its financial statements into a foreign language. Because of some of the issues mentioned earlier concerning social structures and other cultural barriers, this is not unproblematic. After all, it is unlikely that real equivalence will be achieved in translation. Some companies, such as Montedison, make this clear when they describe their English-language version as a 'free translation of the Italian text'.

The question is: 'what is lost and what is gained in translation?' Some companies indicate an awareness of the potential pitfalls that can arise in international financial communication, where translation from a source language to another language occurs. For example, in the English language version of their financial report, one leading Dutch company notes that 'in the event of a conflict in interpretation, reference should be made to the Dutch version of this Annual Report' and one of the German multinationals makes an even bolder declaration in its English language report, disclaiming responsibility for translation equivalence: 'the auditors' report applies to the *German* version of the Financial Statements and Business Report'.

One of the reasons for this concern about equivalence in translation is that accounting terminology is particularly idiomatic. Terms like 'Net Working Capital' or 'Liquid Funds' are charged with idiosyncratic meaning which may well be shared by the professional community which takes an interest in financial reporting but which is something of an obstacle to others. Even for the professional analyst, the language barrier is a significant problem in international financial analysis. After all, when we consider the phrase 'true and fair view', the English analyst has to travel no further than to France before meeting the surrealistic notion of '*une image fidèle*', to be contrasted with the momentary snapshot implied by '*ein Blick*' in some audit reports attached to German financial statements!

In fact, we meet a similar problem with financial ratio terminology. The German *Innenfinanzierungsspielraum* implicates both the notion of 'internal financing' and that of 'capacity', as indeed it is the ratio of Operating Cash Flow to New Investment. We find an equally idiomatic version in the French *taux d'autofinancement*, but the notion of 'self-financing' is not in common use in English. In some cases, the idiom is preserved in translation, as in the French *Rotation des Stocks* (Stock Turnover), and there are other cases where the metaphor is shared such as *Anspannungskoeffizient* which conveys in German the Newtonian notion of Leverage (i.e. Gearing, or Total Debt to Capital Employed). However, French speakers will be aware of the influence of the *Académie Française*, and will not be surprised to hear of the entry in the Official Journal of the Republic where, in addition to pointing out that *le software* would be more appropriately described as *le logiciel*, it was noted that the preferred version of *le PE ratio* is now *le coefficient de capitalisation des résultats*. What further evidence could be required to demonstrate that foreign financial terminology is in reality a Trojan horse which brings with it its own social structures and cultural connotations than the reactions of the guardians of the purity of the French language!

Disclosure of Financial Ratios

There is frequent reference to financial ratios in published annual reports and, in some countries, it is usual for a set of ratio indicators to be published. In Figure 7.2, an extract from the report of Esselte illustrates this disclosure practice, which is adopted by a number of Swedish companies.

There has been pressure to introduce sets of standardised reported ratios elsewhere, and one reason given is that the information needed for uniform computation may not be available in a company's annual report. Another reason is that information intermediaries frequently use different formulas for ratios with similar descriptions. In the USA, for instance, in *Annual Statement Studies* published by Robert Morris Associates, inventory turnover is computed by dividing cost of sales by inventory, whilst in 'Ratios of Manufacturing' published in Dun's Review, the inventory turnover ratio is computed by dividing net sales by inventory (see Gibson, 1980). But there is also considerable inconsistency in the way companies compute the ratios which they choose to disclose. For instance, from a sample of 100 companies, Gibson reported eight ways in which the Profit Margin is computed. Furthermore, there are obvious preferences for particular key ratios. Using broad categorisations, the ranking in Table 7.7 was obtained by Gibson:

Table 7.7 Disclosure of Ratios

Ratio	*Frequency of disclosure*
Return on equity	62
Profit margin	58
Current ratio	47
Debt to capital	23
Return on capital	21
Debt to equity	19

There is also evidence of selective reporting by companies. Perhaps the point to be emphasised here is that the 'self-interest' of managers may affect the scope and computation of financial indicators published by a company (Foster, 1986), and that the response of analysts could well be to ignore the summary indicators published by companies.

7.5 Analysts' Earnings Adjustments

There is one financial ratio where there is widespread recognition of the need for a standard computation: Earnings Per Share. Along with other aspects of financial reporting in Europe, the calculation of EPS was investigated by the Global Research Group at UBS–Phillips & Drew (1987). Some of their findings are summarised below, revealing that, even in the case of this commonly-used and commonly-reported indicator, the method of calculation varies considerably from country to country:

Definitions of financial ratios

Return on capital employed, before tax
'Operating income after depreciation' plus financial income as a percentage of average total assets, excluding interest-free operating liabilities.

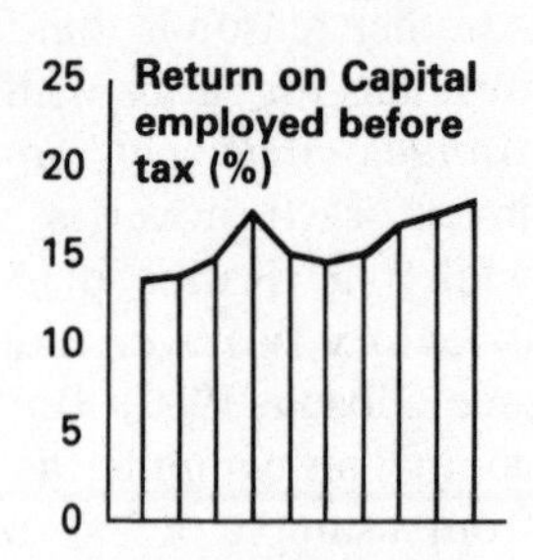

Return on stockholders' equity, after tax
'Income after net interest expense' less estimated taxes as a percentage of average stockholders' equity, calculated as the sum of shareholders' equity and untaxed reserves less deferred tax liability.

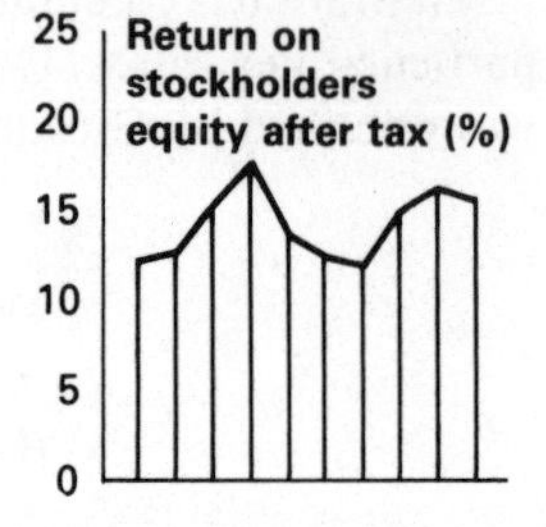

In calculating the return on stockholders' equity, both an estimated 'actual' tax based on the partial-tax method and a theoretical tax based on the full-tax method are used.

Under the partial-tax method, reported taxes for the year are increased by taxes on appropriations that are expected to be recovered within three years, or appropriations that involve deposits in interest-free blocked accounts in the Bank of Sweden, etc. When untaxed reserves are withdrawn, they are taxed to the extent that they have not been taxed at the time the appropriations were made, as described above. The amount added to reported taxes to cover taxes on the untaxed reserves/appropriations is based on a tax rate of 50 per cent.

Under the full-tax method, a theoretical tax is based on the assumption that all untaxed reserves must be withdrawn. In principle, actual tax rates have been used in the countries affected.

The untaxed reserves in the capital base have been reduced by the amount of the deferred tax liability calculated in accordance with the two methods noted above.

For comparability with previous years, the calculation is also made in accordance with a standard method of taxation, assuming a tax rate of 50 per cent.

Return on risk capital, before tax
'Income after net interest expense' as a percentage of average risk capital calculated as the sum of shareholders' equity, minority interest and untaxed reserves.

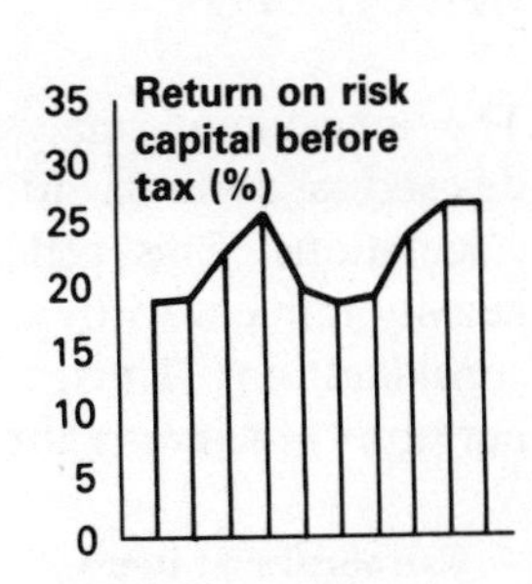

Net income per share
'Income after net interest expense' — excluding minority interests — less estimated taxes, divided by the number of shares outstanding. The number of shares has been adjusted to reflect stock dividends and new issues of shares.

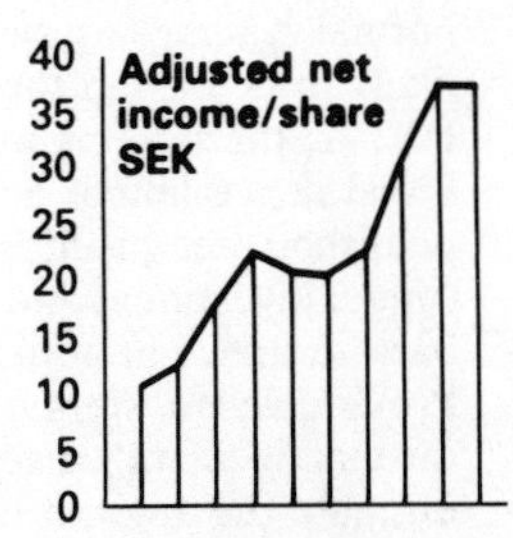

Return on sales
'Operating income after depreciation' plus financial income, as a percentage of total sales.

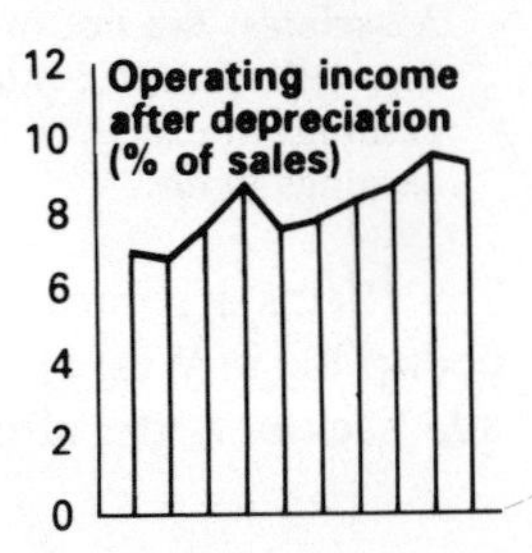

Equity/assets ratio
Shareholders' equity, minority interest and 50 per cent of untaxed reserves as a percentage of total assets.

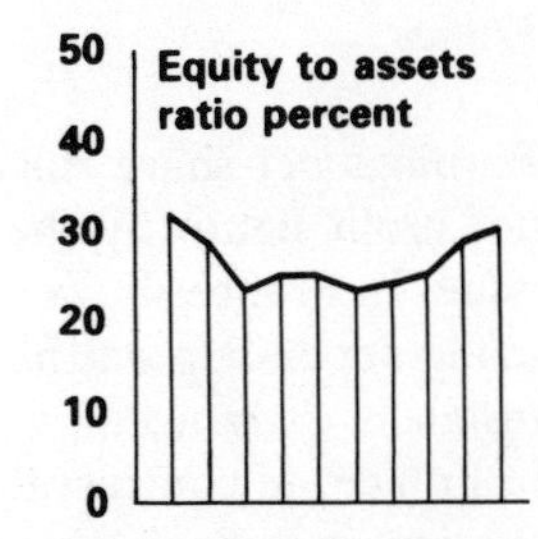

Borrowing/risk capital ratio
Total borrowed capital including pension liabilities (interest-bearing liabilities) as a percentage of total risk capital.

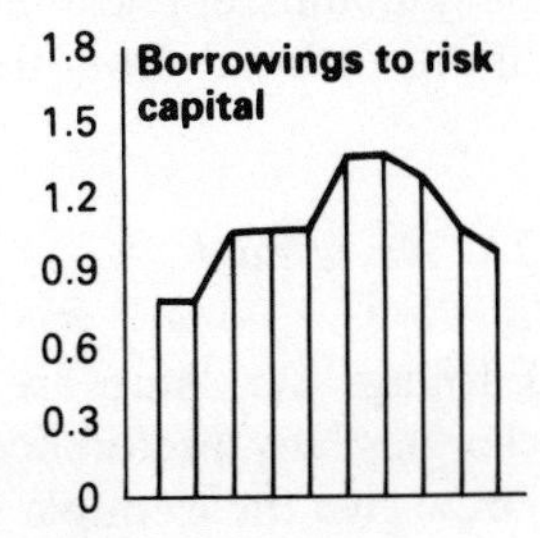

Figure 7.2 Ratio Disclosure by Esselte

West Germany

The investment analysts' association in West Germany (DVFA) has devised a formula to arrive at adjusted profit figures used in EPS calculations. This reflects the fact that published earnings figures are heavily influenced by compliance with legal requirements and with fiscal considerations. Thus, a number of adjustments are made to the published net profit, including the following:

Extraordinary items: income and expenditure incurred outside the company's normal trading, as well as items relating to activities in prior periods, are likely to be passed through the Income Statement. As recommended by the DVFA, these items will be excluded from adjusted earnings.
Fiscal depreciation: a number of tax allowances are deducted in computing published net profit such as accelerated depreciation on certain types of capital investment and reductions in the valuation of stocks. These are added back to arrive at adjusted earnings.
Provisions: transfers to medium and long-term provisions are carried out at the management's discretion and, in this case, it will probably be necessary to estimate the amount of the adjustment that has to be made.
Associates: the net profit disclosed by German companies does not include the attributable earnings of associates, and therefore the share in associate earnings in excess of dividends received will be incorporated in the adjusted earnings figure.

Tax effects are important here. For example, pension provisions are tax-deductible in West Germany and therefore it is recommended by DVFA to add back only the after-tax amount. An example is given in Table 7.8.

France

Earnings per share calculations are commonly performed by dividing the net profit figure by the weighted average number of ordinary shares in issue. In France, however, there are a number of adjustments that can be made depending on the extent of the financial information available. For instance, extraordinary items are not distinguished from exceptional items in France, in contrast to UK practice. An investor should try to establish the amounts applicable to each category, and exclude the extraordinary profits or losses from the earnings per share calculations.

The Netherlands

Earnings per share are calculated after extraordinary items and before charging any preference dividend. In their monograph, UBS-Phillips & Drew give the example shown in Table 7.9 for the Dutch publisher VNU.

Table 7.8 Calculation of Earnings According to the DFVA Method: Example Based on Thyssen's Annual Report

DMm			*Net of tax adjustment*	*Adjusted earnings*	*Source*
Published net profit for the year				472	P&L
Profit from disposal & revaluation of fixed assets	49				P&L
Write back of provisions	201				P&L
Write back of tax-free reserves	130				P&L
	380	@ 37.5%	−142		
Investment grants			−122		Notes
Total of extraordinary & prior year adjustments to be excluded			−264	−264	
Write down of current assets	107				P&L
Loss on disposal of fixed assets	98				P&L
Additions to tax-free reserves	1				P&L
Capital raising costs	15				Estimate
Total of extraordinary and prior year adjuments to be included	221	@ 37.5%		+ 83	
Write down of financial assets	51				P&L
Special depreciation	89				Notes
Net increase in pension provisions	186				Balance sheet
Net increase in other medium and long-term provisions	97				Estimate
Total other adjustments	423	@ 37.5%		+158	
Minorities				− 23	
DVFA net profit				426	
Average number of shares in issue (m)				3.13	
Adjusted EPS				13.6	

Table 7.9 Calculation of Earnings per Share by VNU (in Guilders 000)

		Stated EPS	*Adjusted EPS*
Pre-tax profits		101,072	101,072
Income taxes		(35,269)	(35,269)
Extraordinary loss		(5,504)	
Preference dividends			(210)
Tax benefit		5,249	5,249
Net Earnings		**65,548**	**70,842**
Weighted number of shares	2,713,000		
Earnings per share		**24.16**	**26.11**

Sweden

There is no legal requirement to disclose Earnings Per Share in Sweden, but most listed companies do. As mentioned earlier, tax adjustments are important, as taxable profits depend on appropriations to special investment reserves. The effect is shown in the example for Electrolux in 1985 (see Table 7.10). We can compare the actual tax EPS and the standard tax EPS over a ten-year period in Figure 7.3.

Table 7.10 Calculation of Earnings per Share by Electrolux (in Swedish Kr. 000)

	Income statement	*Actual tax*	*Full tax*	*Standard tax*
Profit before extraordinary items	2576			2576
Extraordinary items	176			—
	2752	**2752**	**2752**	**2576**
Appropriations to reserves	(593)	—	—	—
Minorities (before tax)	—	—	—	(33)
Profit before tax	**2159**	**2752**	**2752**	**2543**
Tax	(749)	(749)	(749)	(1271)
Tax on reserves	—	—	(296)	—
Profit after tax	**1410**	**2003**	**1707**	**1272**
Minorities (after tax)	(15)	(19)	(17)	—
Net Earnings	**1395**	**1984**	**1690**	**1272**
Number of shares	65.5m	65.5m	65.5m	65.5m
Earnings per share	**21.3**	**30.3**	**25.8**	**19.4**

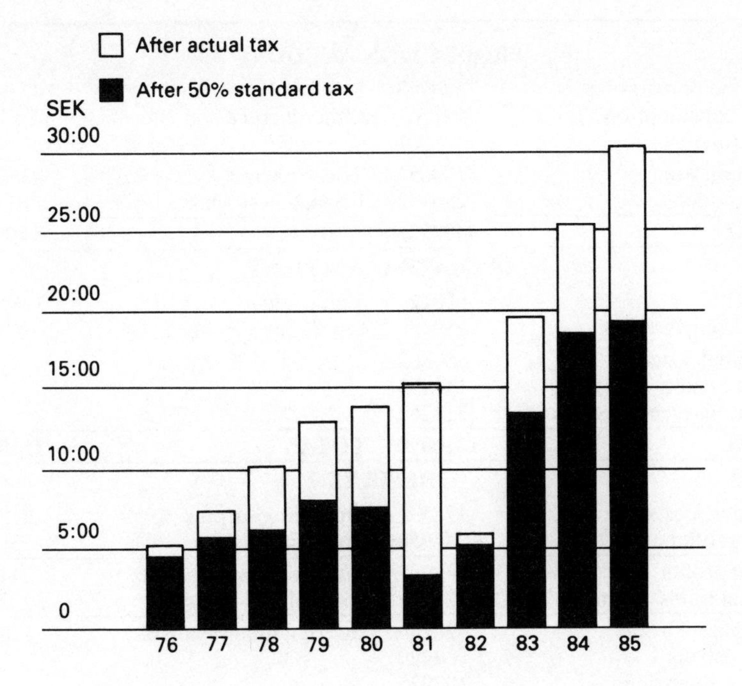

Figure 7.3 Earnings per Share Disclosed by Electrolux

7.6 Estimating Country Effects

One way of placing a company in its operating context is to compare financial ratios for the company in question with aggregate indicators for the economy as a whole. These benchmark ratios may serve as characteristic values for the economy, and thus provide a way of assessing the 'country effect', i.e. the mean effect for all companies operating within that economy.

Economic and statistical institutes are a major source of such information. For instance, in France, the organisation which co-ordinates national economic accounting (INSEE) publishes consolidated financial statements for the corporate sector, with segmentation by industry, by firm size, and by region. In France, the amount of financial information that is made available in this way is extensive, and the Intermediary Accounts which result from an extensive social consolidation of financial disclosures by French companies are not usually subject to great delay as is sometimes the case with this sort of large-scale statistical analysis. The financial ratios which are published by INSEE are shown in Table 7.11.

Table 7.11 The Intermediary Accounts for the French Corporate Sector

PRODUCTION ACCOUNT

Purchase of materials	2500983	Sales and own construction	4289594
Other consumption	691567	Other income	71158
Adjustment	1501		
Consumption	3194051	Total revenue	4360752
Value added	1286872	Change in stocks	120171
TOTAL	**4480923**	**TOTAL**	**4480923**

OPERATING ACCOUNT

Salaries	630424	Value added	1286872
Social contributions	250438	Operating subsidies	23226
Personnel costs	880862		
Indirect taxes	110953		
Operating surplus	318283		
TOTAL	**1310098**	**TOTAL**	**1310098**

RESULTS

Financing costs	128531	Operating surplus	318283
Gross profit before tax	244958	Financial income	55206
Tax on profits	48967	Gross profits before tax	244958
Internal funds available	228585	Exceptional items	32594
Distributed profits	26240	Internal funds available	228585
Profit sharing	4420		
Internal financing	197925		

BALANCE SHEET

Deferred charges	45565	Share capital	406345
less amortisation	−26224	Revaluation reserves	100557
	19341	Revaluation provisions	63144
Fixed assets	1782278	Capital and reserves	878882
less depreciation	−788229	Capital investment grants	21746
	994049	Sundry provisions	117529
Other long-term assets	493422	Current profits	89388
less provisions	−45914	Current losses	−50854
	447508	Shareholders equity	1056691
		Long-term debt	692308
Long-term assets	**1460898**	**Long-term capital**	**1748999**
Stocks	781706		
less provisions	−19999		
	761707		
Accounts receivable	711634	Accounts payable	920122
Cash and banks	176083	Bank overdrafts	107199
Other short-term assets	443691	Other short-term liabilities	777682
Current assets	**1331408**	**Current liabilities**	**1805003**
Adjustment	−11		
TOTAL	**3554002**	**TOTAL**	**3554002**

Table 7.11 (continued)

RATIOS	
Value Added/Total Revenue	0,2951
Value Added/Fixed Assets	0,7220
Depreciation/Fixed Assets	0,4422
Personnel Costs/Personnel Costs & Operating Surplus	0,7345
Operating Surplus/Total Revenue	0,0729
Operating Surplus/Fixed Assets	0,1785
Internal Funds Available/Shareholders' Equity	0,2163
Long-term Capital/Long-term Assets	1,1972
Long-term Debt/Shareholders' Equity	0,6551
Total Revenue/Average Stock	6,1958
Sales/Trade Debtors	6,7372
Purchases/Trade Creditors	28,572
Long-term Debt/Sales	0,1613
Internal Financing/New Investment & Change in Stocks	0,5551

However, analysts are likely to have at their disposal a number of sources of such benchmarks. For instance, the *Centrale de Bilans* at the *Banque de France* also publishes statistical summaries of the financial results of French companies, including average ratios for different sectors and for different sizes of company. Moreover, given the rapid development of electronic financial information networks, industry and economy-wide statistics are readily available. Information intermediaries such as Datastream in the UK can provide aggregate indicators which are continually updated as new results are published.

But care should be taken when drawing inferences about 'mean effects' within a given country (or within a sector within a country) using the commercial financial information services, as the benchmarks in question are often obtained from sub-populations which have not been constructed for this purpose. Also, there is an important theoretical issue here. A ratio computed from social accounts is a ratio of economic aggregates (which, of course, is equal to the ratio of the means of those macroeconomic quantities), but this is unlikely to be equal to the average ratio for companies in the sector or economy. These differences can be important, as the illustrative results for French textile companies show in Table 7.12.

Table 7.12 Return on Capital Employed in the French Textiles Sector

	Mean ratio $\frac{1}{n}\Sigma(Y_i/X_i)$	*Ratio of means* $\frac{1}{n}\Sigma Y_i/\frac{1}{n}\Sigma X_i$
1980	15.2	12.7
1981	15.8	12.6
1982	17.2	15.0
1983	17.0	15.1

Indeed, in a study of 15 different indicators, McLeay and Fieldsend (1987) found that the behaviour of financial ratios is such that these differences are important in most cases, and depend on such aspects of industrial structure as the size distribution of firms. The question that arises is this: 'how do we obtain a reliable estimate of the 'country effect'?'

Ratio Models

One way of solving the above problem is to consider statistical models which may be used to provide more robust estimators of characteristic values for financial ratios and to allow for effects attributable to the nature of the operating environment (country effects) as well as other important effects such as those attributable to the type of industrial activity (sector effects). In this way, information may be provided about inter-relationships between companies, between sectors and between nations.

Here, a comparison between Japanese, US and UK firms provides insight into this approach, and is carried out within a bivariate lognormal variance component analysis. For illustration, the indicator that is investigated here is the Current Ratio whose distribution is positive, the ratio in question being computed from two underlying positively distributed variables, Current Assets (CA) and Current Liabilities (CL). For this example, the regression model is specified as:

$$lnCA = \alpha + \beta lnCL$$

where for $\beta = 1$ we have

$$lnCA - lnCL = \alpha$$

and, accordingly, the expected value of the Current Ratio is given by:

$$CA/CL = e^{\alpha}$$

Now, for the ith company in the jth sector in the kth country, we have:

$$lnCA_{ijk} = \alpha + \alpha_j + \alpha_k + \beta lnCL_{ijk} + \beta_j lnCL_{ijk} + \beta_k lnCL_{ijk} + \epsilon_{ijk}$$

which reduces to:

$$CA_{ijk}/CL_{ijk} = \exp(\alpha + \alpha_j + \alpha_k + \epsilon_{ijk})$$

when β is equal to 1 and the within-sector effects β_j and the within-country effects β_k exhibit no variance, and where:

α is the geometric mean for all companies,
α_j is an effect attributable to the sector of operations which is a variable

intercept term described here as the between-sector effect,
α_k is the between-country effect, and
ϵ_{ijk} is the residual company effect, i.e. the extent to which the company's ratio departs from the norm after taking account of differences between sectors and differences between countries.

A comparison of mean and median Current Ratios is given in Table 7.13. It is based on information from Datastream and, for this analysis, Current Asset and Current Liability figures were obtained for companies operating in seven major sectors in the USA, the UK and Japan. The samples are not balanced, but they comprise all listed companies in the three countries in question whose principal operations are in electronics, electricals, mechanical engineering, motor manufacturing, food manufacturing, textiles and chemicals.

The differences between countries in the median ratio are shown clearly in the table, and the persistence of the differences from year to year is also evident. Also, it can be seen that the arithmetic mean is higher than the median in each case, reflecting the skewed positive distribution of the Current Ratio.

Table 7.13 Current Ratio: International Differences

		Mean	*Median*
USA	1984	2.881	2.375
	1985	2.980	2.385
	1986	2.877	2.363
UK	1984	1.699	1.563
	1985	1.661	1.540
	1986	1.672	1.575
Japan	1984	1.390	1.232
	1985	1.418	1.264
	1986	1.554	1.305

Mean and median ratios for quoted companies operating in the following sectors: electronics, electricals, mechanical engineering, motor manufacturing, food manufacturing, textiles and chemicals.

Analysis

The variance component analysis was first carried out separately for each country, with sector effects being added by allowing:

(i) a random intercept term α_j to vary from sector to sector, in the between-sector effects model

$$lnCA_{ij} = \alpha + \alpha_j + \beta lnCL_{ij} + \epsilon_{ij}$$

Table 7.14 Variance Component Analysis of the Current Ratio: Estimates, Standard Errors (in brackets) and Deviances

	Overall slope β	*Standard deviations*		*Deviance*	*Reduction in deviance*
		Intercept σ_I	*Slope* σ_S		
UK (469 companies)					
Fixed effects	1.00206 (0.00994)			391.99	
Between-sector effects	0.99534 (0.00972)	0.11575 (0.03625)		368.01	−23.98**
Within-sector effects	0.99518 (0.01008)	0.11540 (0.03452)	0.00697 (0.01382)	367.41	−0.60
USA (610 companies)					
Fixed effects	1.07832 (0.01302)			893.85	
Between-sector effects	1.06607 (0.01301)	0.10279 (0.03621)		878.90	−16.95**
Within-sector effects	1.06643 (0.01388)	0.10390 (0.03643)	0.00994 (0.02737)	878.90	0.00

Japan (352 companies)					
Fixed effects	1.02431 (0.01516)			223.55	
Between-sector effects	1.01861 (0.01486)	0.09962 (0.03227)		200.74	−22.81**
Within-sector effects	1.02073 (0.01697)	0.09485 (0.02621)	0.02149 (0.01830)	197.18	−3.56*
Combined data (1431 companies)					
Fixed effects	1.02234 (0.00742)			2127.36	
Between-country effects	1.03932 (0.00739)	0.26843 (0.11020)		1645.33	−482.03**
Between-sector effects	1.01726 (0.00731)	0.12435 (0.03608)		2043.33	−84.03**§
Between-sector and between-country effects	1.03148 (0.00731)	0.09968 (0.02920)		1575.81	−551.55**§
Within-sector and between-country effects	1.03326 (0.00937)	0.10148 (0.02919)	0.01518 (0.00876)	1574.36	−1.45
Within-sector and within-country effects	1.03019 (0.01185)	0.09957 (0.02102)	0.03943 (0.01063)	1561.86	−12.50**

Notes: ** *highly significant,* **significant,* § *reduction from fixed effects.*

(ii) both a random intercept term α_j and a random slope term β_j to vary from sector to sector in the within-sector effects model

$$lnCA_{ij} = \alpha + \alpha_j + \beta lnCL_{ij} + \beta_j lnCL_{ij} + \epsilon_{ij}$$

The results of the first analysis are presented at the top of Table 7.14. In fact, there is mixed support for the hypothesis of ratio proportionality, and only for UK companies is there strong support for the hypothesis that 1 is a plausible value for β. For Japanese companies, the β coefficient is greater than 1 in each case, although the standard errors permit the inference of proportionality at a relatively weak level. However, for US companies, there is an obvious size effect, with β significantly greater than 1 for each regression.

However, our initial interest is in the difference in Current Ratio values between sectors. Again, looking at the results for each country subset at the top of Table 7.14, it will be seen that by allowing the intercept to vary between sectors, there is a substantial reduction in deviance (−2 loglikelihood) which is highly significant by comparison with the relevant F-statistic (e.g. the deviance falls by 23.98 from 391.99 to 368.01 in the case of UK companies). The variability of the sector intercepts is also evidenced by their standard deviation σ_I which could not plausibly be zero. But there is little evidence of within-sector effects, as the change in deviance when sector regression slopes are allowed to vary is small (e.g. from 368.01 to 367.41 for UK companies). The high ratios of standard error to the estimate of the variability of the sector slope coefficient σ_S supports this inference.

At this stage, we conclude that sector differences are extremely important within each of the three countries.

In the next variance component analysis, the three data sets are combined and relative contributions of sector differences and country differences are investigated by allowing:

(i) the intercept to vary between countries only, where it can be seen that a massive reduction in deviance is achieved;
(ii) the intercept to vary between sectors only, where there is a substantial contribution to explanation, but far less than the between-country effects;
(iii) the intercept to vary between sectors and between countries, in what is a relatively parsimonious model for this very large data set, including just three country intercepts and seven sector intercepts —

$$lnCA_{ijk} = \alpha + \alpha_j + \alpha_k + \beta lnCL_{ijk} + \epsilon_{ijk}$$

also, finally, by permitting random slopes:

(i) for sectors only, which adds nothing to the explanatory model;
(ii) for both sectors and countries, which tells us that there are significant differences in ratio proportionality between countries, as mentioned before, but which is relatively unimportant by comparison with the differences between countries and between sectors.

Conclusion

The final conclusion is this: for the example given here, international differences in corporate Current Ratios are substantial, and they are far more significant than differences between sectors. For instance (and in spite of the small number of groupings used here), a review of the sector benchmarks obtained with each of these models revealed some stability across countries, with the Current Ratios of motor manufacturers generally being the highest in each country.

These results might be compared with the statistics reported by Choi *et al.* (1983) (see Table 7.3) where Current Ratios of Japanese and US companies were shown to differ significantly (the difference in levels will be due to a number of factors: (i) the use here of more recent data but restricted to only seven sectors, (ii) differences in the source of the data and, possibly, in accounting method, and (iii) the use of different statistical estimators). However, Choi *et al.* demonstrated that accounting restatement using US GAAP for Japanese companies had little effect in explaining the inter-country differences which they observed, and therefore that there are important differences between company liquidity in the US and Japan as measured by this indicator.

There is a final and important point to note. In the analysis reported here, the residual *inter-company* variability is substantial, accounting for about 75 per cent of the total deviance. This suggests that major explanations will be obtained either by including additional explanatory variables, or through financial analysis at the level of the individual firm, both within countries and internationally.

7.7 Summary

In this chapter, it has been argued that proper account must be taken in international financial analysis of the effects of the local operating environment on a company's reported results. Somehow or other, the analyst needs to be able to allow for the effects that are attributable to the company's country of operations in assessing the residual performance or structure of the company itself. Of course, it is also necessary to allow for differences in accounting method, but it has been shown that to some extent the latter may well be a function of, and will even interact with, the social system(s) and financial system(s) within which a company operates. Some companies respond to this by providing information that might assist the foreign user of accounts to understand the particularities of national accounting rules and tax legislation, and other matters such as the constraints of local financing.

In the final section, an approach to statistical modelling has been introduced which attempts to deal analytically with the problem of quantifying these 'country effects' in the context of financial statement analysis.

References

Archer, G.S.H. and McLeay, S.J. (1987) 'Les rapports financiers des sociétés européennes cotées dans différents pays: problèmes liés à la présentation de l'information et aux travaux d'audit', *Revue Française de Comptabilité*, June, pp. 48–61.

Arnold, J. and Moizer, P. (1984) 'A survey of the methods used by UK investment analysts to appraise investments in ordinary shares', *Accounting and Business Research*, Summer, pp. 195–207.

Chang, L.S., Most, K.S. and Brain, C.W. (1983) 'The utility of annual reports: an international study', *Journal of International Business Studies*, Spring/Summer, pp. 63–84.

Choi, F.D.S. *et al.* (1983) 'Analysing foreign financial statements: the use and misuse of international ratio analysis', *Journal of International Business Studies*, Spring/Summer, pp. 113–131.

Day, J.F.S. (1986) 'The use of annual reports by UK investment analysts', *Accounting and Business Research*, Autumn, pp. 295–307.

Foster, G. (1986) *Financial Statement Analysis*, Prentice-Hall.

Gibson, C.H. (1980) 'The need for disclosure of uniform financial ratios', *Journal of Accountancy*, May, pp. 78–84.

Gray, S.J. (1980) 'The impact of international accounting differences from a security-analysis perspective', *Journal of Accounting Research*, Spring, pp. 64–76.

McLeay, S.J., (1983) 'Value added: a comparative study', *Accounting, Organizations and Society*, Vol. 8, No. 1, pp. 31–56.

McLeay, S.J. (1986) 'The ratio of means, the mean of ratios and other benchmarks: an examination of characteristic financial ratios in the French corporate sector', *Finance — the Journal of the French Finance Association*, Vol. 7, No. 1, pp. 75–93.

McLeay, S.J. and Fieldsend, S. (1987) 'Sector and size effects in ratio analysis — an indirect test of ratio proportionality', *Accounting and Business Research*, Spring, pp. 133–140.

UBS Phillips and Drew Global Research Group (1987) *Understanding European Financial Statements*, UBS Phillips and Drew, April.

Further Reading

A recent overview of research in financial statement analysis is given in:

Barnes, P. (1987) 'The analysis and use of financial ratios', *Journal of Business Finance and Accounting*, Winter, pp. 449–461.

A more detailed discussion of the use of variance component analysis can be found in:

Fieldsend, S.P., Longford, N.J. and McLeay, S.J. (1987) 'Industry effects and the proportionality assumption in ratio analysis: a variance component analysis', *Journal of Business Finance and Accounting*, Winter, pp. 497–517.

8
International Transfer Pricing

JEFFREY S. ARPAN

8.1 Introduction

The bulk of international trade in goods and services is conducted by multinational enterprises (MNEs). Furthermore, as noted in studies by the United Nations (1978) and the US Tariff Commission (1973), a large percentage of that international trade conducted by MNEs occurs among the various units of the MNEs themselves, such as between the parent (mother) company and its foreign subsidiaries, or between its subsidiaries in different countries.

One could make a distinction between *intra*-corporate transfer prices and *inter*-corporate transfer prices by using the former to refer to transactions among divisions of a single incorporated entity, and the latter to refer to transactions among different corporate entities of one large company. However, in this chapter *inter-corporate* refers to any transfer made within a global corporate family. Inter-corporate pricing is also used synonymously with transfer pricing.

In its simplest yet broadest sense, inter-corporate pricing is the determination of value for a good or service transferred among business units that share common ownership. It encompasses the determination of interest rates for loans, charges for rentals, fees for services, prices for goods, and the methods of payment. It *excludes* the determination of prices quoted to unaffiliated buyers, although these prices can be both directly and indirectly affected by inter-corporate prices.

International inter-corporate transfers are integral and important activities of MNEs for several reasons. First, raw materials not available or in short supply for an MNE unit in one country can be imported for sale or further processing by another unit of the MNE located in a different country. For example, Reynolds Metal Company's subsidiary in Jamaica exports bauxite to Reynolds US for subsequent processing into aluminium.

Second, some stages of an MNE's production process can be conducted more efficiently in countries other than that where the MNE has its headquarters. For example, to minimise total production costs many MNEs produce or assemble components in lower labour-cost countries. They then ship these components or sub-assemblies to headquarters or subsidiaries in another country for final assembly. A substantial percentage of automobile production takes place in this manner, for instance.

Third, many MNEs operate sales offices in some countries but do no manufacturing there. To sell their products, the sales offices or subsidiaries must import products from manufacturing affiliates in other countries. Or an MNE affiliate may be producing and selling some products in the local market, but also selling products of the MNE that it does not produce locally. For example, it may produce and sell refrigerators locally but import micro-wave ovens for sale locally that are made by a foreign affiliate.

Fourth, many services for MNE units are rendered by MNE headquarters or other affiliates of an MNE. For example, headquarters may conduct research and development for the benefit of all units, develop advertising campaigns for them, or provide them with management consulting. A sales subsidiary typically conducts marketing operations for a manufacturing subsidiary, a manufacturing subsidiary provides production services for a sales subsidiary, and so on.

Finally, there are many international financial flows between units of an MNE. Some are payments related to goods or services provided by other units; some are loans or loan repayments; some are dividends; and some are designed to lessen taxes or financial risks.

Thus, considered collectively, international inter-corporate transfers are a major component of international trade and are vitally important to most MNEs. However, they are also of considerable importance and concern to most governments. As noted most recently in Rugman and Eden (1985) the main reason for governments' interest in international inter-corporate flows is their potential misuse and frequent abuse. More precisely, it is the *pricing* of the inter-corporate transfers that is of greatest concern to governments.

8.2 The Pricing of Inter-Corporate Transfers

Because inter-corporate transfers occur among members of an MNE, their pricing is more open-ended than that for goods and services transferred to or from unaffiliated companies. Theoretically, and often in reality, MNE headquarters can decide and dictate whatever prices it desires, at least in the case of transfers involving wholly-owned affiliates.

Basic Approaches

Although there are hundreds of individual company variations, there are fundamentally two types of transfer pricing systems in use: those based on internal costs and those based on external market prices. The former begin with some internally calculated cost: full cost, variable cost or marginal cost. They then usually add to this a percentage mark-up, such as 10 per cent, which allows a margin of profit to accrue to the seller. Although some companies use different cost bases and percentage mark-ups for different products sold to different affiliates at different times, the 'cost-plus' approach is the same. Transfer prices that are *not* based on cost usually begin with an established market price, such as the posted price for crude oil, but often are sold subsequently at that price minus a percentage discount to allow a margin of profit to the buying unit. The customary justification for such discounts is that the purchaser is doing some product modification or adaptation not usually performed by unaffiliated buyers. Therefore, the affiliate should pay less for the product than those who buy the product in finished form.

Obviously, the derived prices resulting from the two methods converge at some percentage mark-up and mark-down: cost plus 50 per cent equals a market price minus 25 per cent for a good that costs $50 but has a market price of $100. Yet governments and competitors show a marked preference for market-based prices because they are reputedly less arbitrary and therefore fairer. It should be pointed out, however, that market-based prices are not necessarily less arbitrary or more fair than cost-based prices. As observed by Thomas (1971), *both* prices can be highly arbitrary.

On the one hand, all costs are arbitrarily determined, regardless of the accounting system a company uses. If a certain percentage of overheads is allocated to a product, the method of allocation, the percentage allocated, and the very decision to allocate are arbitrary. The only true measure of cost is one that accountants do not as yet know how to measure: the full cost to the society of having the good produced and consumed, including all externalities and all opportunity costs.

On the other hand, transfer prices based on market prices can be just as arbitrary. Market prices reflect true value only when they are determined in a freely competitive market. But in markets where either buyers or sellers influence the market price by changing the quantity supplied or demanded, a degree of arbitrariness is always present. By restricting supply, monopolists can maintain an artificially high price for the products they sell. Alternatively, by refusing to buy at high prices, monopsonists can maintain artificially low prices, and so on.

Thus, as observed by Keegan (1969) and many others, what remain in reality are arbitrary costs and arbitrary market prices. Since both are arbitrary, what matters is their *degree* of arbitrariness — their distance from real value. In this respect, it is often argued that market-based transfer prices are relatively less arbitrary than those based on cost. But at times, and for certain products, even this is not always true. Where there is no true free market for a product, its internally computed cost can conceivably be the best approximation of its real value.

From a company standpoint, cost-based prices have one distinct advantage over market-based prices: flexibility. Because any cost element that enters into the computation of the base price can be changed as well as the percentage mark-up, it is much easier to change a transfer price based on cost than one based on market price. Therefore, as anyone with the makings of a shrewd international accountant will recognise, it is to the advantage of firms that plan to deviate from market prices in their internal transfers to differentiate their products sufficiently.

8.3 Factors Influencing Transfer Price Determination

For a truly multinational enterprise, its overall international competitive position is its major consideration in determining transfer prices. In analysing its global competitive position, an MNE must consider not only the profitability of its operations in domestic and foreign markets, but also the ways in which they affect each other. Figure 8.1 depicts this pattern of interaction. For example, profits from a Japanese subsidiary can be used to finance increased advertising by its British parent; or low transfer prices on components shipped from a Mexican subsidiary to a Japanese subsidiary can lower the latter's manufacturing cost and permit more aggressive external pricing strategies in Japan or raise the profitability of the Japanese subsidiary. Therefore, an MNE must consider how its inter-corporate transfers, their prices, and the competitive positions of its members affect each other in the light of the company's myriad objectives and competitive constraints.

Corporate Goals

MNEs typically have a variety of objectives. Maximising global after-tax profits is, of course, a major goal. Others often include: increasing market share, maintaining employment stability and harmony, being considered the 'best' firm in the industry, minimising conflicts with governments, and being a good corporate citizen. However, not all of these goals are mutually compatible or collectively achievable. For example, achieving employment stability and harmony in one country may mean reducing employment in another country. Or, actions to please the government in one country may upset the government in another country — a

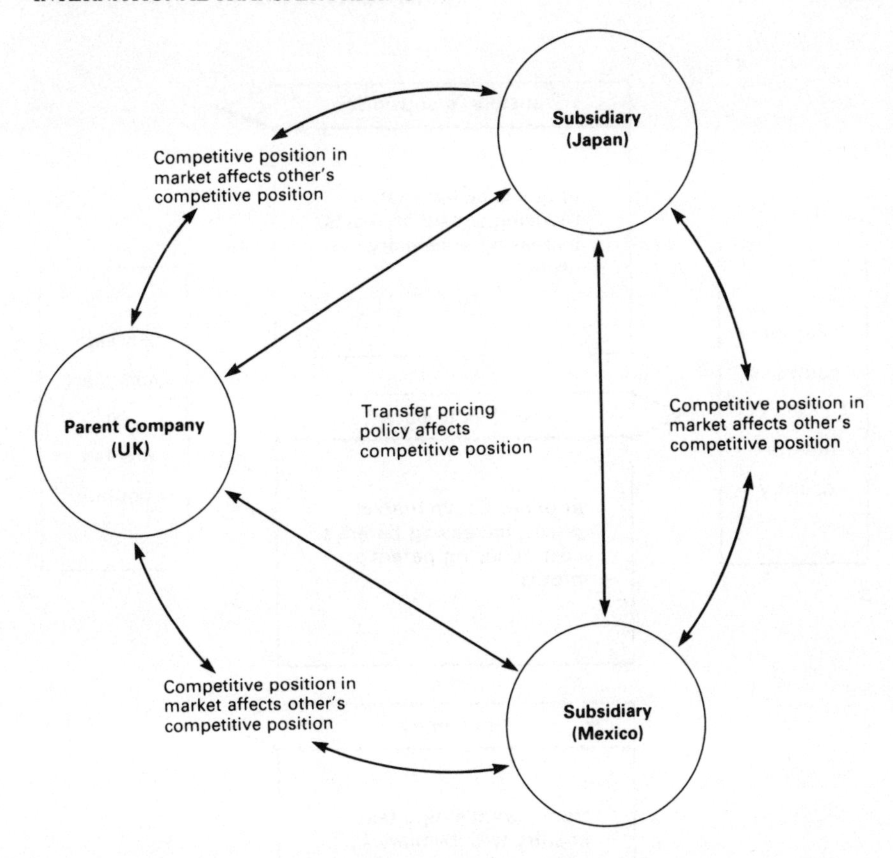

Figure 8.1 Transfer Pricing and Competitive Position

phenomenon likely to occur as a result of adjusting world-wide employment or research and development activities.

In addition, all MNEs face governmental and other constraints which influence their ability to achieve their objectives in the manner they would prefer. Illustrative examples include government restrictions on international flows of information, funds and products, and different competitive conditions in the markets in which an MNE operates. In sum, in determining international inter-corporate transfers and their prices, an MNE must also consider both its goals and the constraints it faces.

Uses of Transfer Pricing to Achieve Corporate Goals

The goal most commonly mentioned, maximisation of global after-tax profits, deserves first scrutiny. It is frequently alleged that multinational companies astutely use their transfer pricing system to maximise profits in

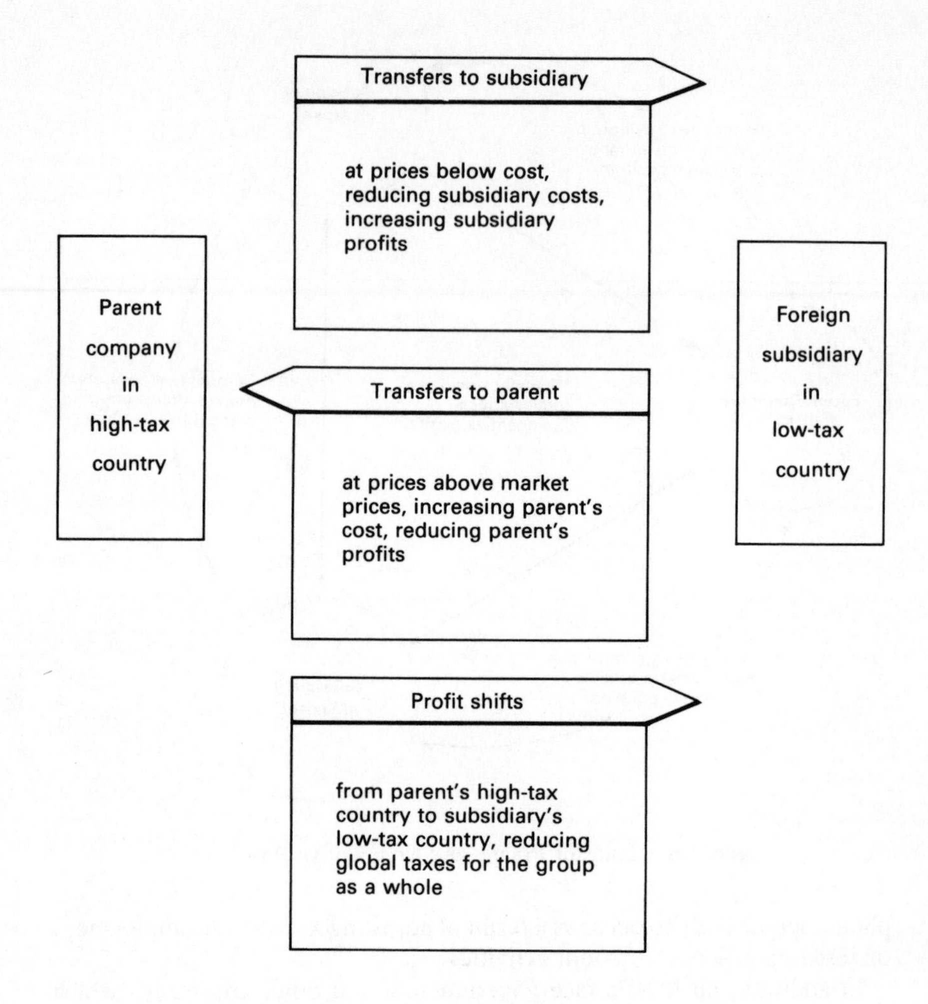

Figure 8.2 Transfer Prices, Taxes and Profits

low-tax countries and minimise them in high-tax countries. Theoretically and actually, this goal can be achieved by using inter-corporate pricing, as depicted in Figure 8.2.

What makes global after-tax profits variable, even *without* transfer price manipulation, is differences in nations' taxation rates and methods. Tax rates on corporate income range from zero to over 70 per cent. Some countries tax dividend distributions while others do not. Some types of income that are considered taxable in some countries are excluded from taxation in other countries, and, in general, the accounting methods for determining taxable income vary widely among countries (Nobes and

Parker, 1985, Ch. 15). As a result, an MNE may choose to make an investment in a particular country in order to take advantage of its lower tax rate, and thereby increase corporate after-tax income.

An MNE can also achieve further tax savings by manipulating its transfer prices to and from its subsidiaries. In effect, it can manoeuvre taxable income out of a high-tax country into a lower-tax country. This tax scheme can be particularly profitable for MNEs based in a country that taxes only income earned in that country but does not tax income earned *outside* the country (France is an example). But even if a country taxes the global income of its corporations (as the USA does), often income earned abroad is not taxable by the country of the corporate parent until it is remitted to the parent. By delaying remittance, MNEs can defer taxation by the parent company's government and, in the interim, make productive use of the taxes deferred. However, it should be noted that many tax authorities carefully scrutinise international transfers and their prices to ascertain whether tax evasion is their objective or result. If it is, an MNE is likely to find itself in court in one or more countries!

If penetrating a foreign market is a company goal, part of the transfer pricing system depicted in Figure 8.2 can also be used effectively. Companies can underprice goods sold to foreign affiliates, and the affiliates can then sell them at prices which their local competitors cannot match. And if anti-dumping laws exist on final products, a company can underprice components and semi-finished products to its affiliates. The affiliates can then assemble or finish the final product at prices that would have been classified as dumping prices had they been imported directly into the country rather than produced inside.

Transfer prices can be used in a similar manner to reduce the impact of tariffs. *Ad valorem* tariffs increase import prices and apply to inter-corporate transfers as well as to sales to unaffiliated buyers. Although no company can do much to change a tariff, the effect of tariffs can be lessened if the selling company underprices the goods it exports to the buying company. For example, consider a product that normally sells for $100 and has an import price of $120 because of a 20 per cent tariff. If the invoice price were listed as $80 rather than $100, it could be imported for $96. The underpricing of inter-corporate transfers can also be used to get more products into a country that is rationing its currency or otherwise limiting the value of goods that can be imported. A subsidiary can import twice as many products if they can be bought at half price.

In other cases, artificially *high* transfer prices can be used to circumvent or lessen significantly the impact of national controls. A government prohibition on dividend remittances to foreign owners can restrict the ability of a firm to manoeuvre income out of a country. However, overpricing the goods shipped to a subsidiary in such a country makes it possible for funds to be taken out. High transfer prices can also be of considerable value to a firm if it is paid a subsidy or earns a tax credit on the value of goods it exports. The higher the transfer prices on exported goods, the greater the subsidy earned or tax credit received.

High transfer prices on goods shipped to subsidiaries can also be desirable when a parent wishes to lower the apparent profitability of its subsidiary. This may be because of demands by the subsidiary's workers for higher wages or participation in company profits, or because of political pressures to expropriate high-profit foreign-owned operations, or because of the possibility that new competitors will be lured into the industry by high profits. There may also be inducements for having high-priced transfers to the subsidary when a joint venture is involved, the inducement being that the increase in the parent company profits will not have to be split with the subsidiary's joint venture partner. High transfer prices may also be desired when increases from existing price controls in the subsidiary's country are based on production costs (costs that include high transfer prices for purchases).

Transfer pricing can also be used to minimise losses from foreign currency fluctuations, or shift losses to particular affiliates. By dictating the specific currency used for payment, the parent determines whether the buying or the selling unit has the exchange risk. Altering the terms and timing of payments and the volume of shipments causes transfer pricing to affect the net foreign exchange exposure of the firm.

Table 8.1 summarises particular conditions that make it advantageous for firms to use a particular level of transfer price. The maximum advantage can be gained when all these conditions line up on a country basis. For example, the parent operates from a country with the characteristics calling for high transfer prices coming in and low transfer prices going out.

Consider the left side of Table 8.1. If the parent sells at low prices to the subsidiary and buys from it at high prices, income is shifted to the subsidiary, lessening the global tax burden. At the same time, the impact of the high *ad valorem* tariffs in the subsidiary's country is lessened and the financial appearance of the subsidiary is enhanced for local borrowing purposes. In addition, the impact of foreign exchange rationing on imports from the parent and dividend payments to the parent are lessened, the subsidiary's ability to penetrate its local market is enhanced, the parent is less affected by its government's restrictions on capital outflows, and so on.

Under this set of conditions, the subsidiary's country gains somewhat more than the parent's: more funds, more taxable income, greater economic growth of the subsidiary, and more export revenues. It loses somewhat in other areas, however: local competitors may suffer adversely, have lower profits, pay less taxes and lay off workers, if the foreign subsidiary actively pursues a market penetration strategy. The government also pays greater subsidies or gives more tax credits because of the

Table 8.1 Conditions in Subsidiary's Country Affecting the Level of Transfer Prices

Conditions in subsidiary's country inducing **low transfer prices** *on flows from parent and* **high transfer prices** *on flows to parent*	*Conditions in subsidiary's country inducing* **high transfer prices** *on flows from parent and* **low transfer prices** *on flows to parent*
High *ad valorem* tariffs	Local partners
Corporate income tax rate lower than in parent's country	Pressure from workers to obtain greater share of company profit
Significant competition	Political pressure to nationalise or expropriate high-profit foreign firms
Local loans based on financial appearance of subsidiary	Restrictions on profit or dividend remittances
Export subsidy or tax credit on value of exports	Political instability
Lower inflation rate than in parent's country	Substantial tie-in sales agreements
Restrictions (ceilings) in subsidiary's country on the value of products that can be imported	Price of final product controlled by government but based on production cost
	Desire to mask profitability of subsidiary operations to keep competitors out

Source: Arpan (1972)

subsidiary's artificially high value of exports and, like the government of the other country, has its national control lessened.

Unfortunately for firms, seldom do the conditions line up as nicely from their standpoint as depicted on either side of Table 8.1. It is far more likely that a country simultaneously will have conditions taken from both sides of the table. For example, a country experiencing balance of payments difficulties typically would be restricting dividend outflows *and* the amount or value of imports. A company using high transfer prices on sales to its subsidiary in such a country would gain in terms of taking out more money than it might have been able to otherwise, but would lose by having to decrease the quantity of imported materials its affiliate needs to compete. Alternatively, a country may have high *ad valorem* tariffs and high income tax rates. Underpricing goods shipped to an affiliate in such a country lessens the tariff duties but also increases subsidiary profits due to lower input costs, resulting in higher taxes for the subsidiary. Therefore, in situations where a country has conditions taken from both sides of Table 8.1, the company must weigh the gains and losses from using a particular level of transfer prices.

So far it is the problems relating to a two-country model that have been discussed. As countries are added, the problems and headaches of transfer pricing grow geometrically. To begin to appreciate the complexity of a multi-country model, refer back to Figure 8.1 and assume that each of the three countries has a set of conditions taken from each side of Table 8.1. Theoretically, and realistically, the multinational's management should weigh the overall gains and losses from each shipment and transfer price for each member, and their impact on the MNE as a whole. But, as Rutenberg (1970) and Lessard (1985) have observed, doing this is not easy. In addition, when we recognise that the specific combination of environmental conditions changes in each country over time, we begin to understand why the effort of constantly re-evaluating and changing intercorporate pricing strategies becomes truly gargantuan.

Other Internal Factors Affecting Transfer Pricing

If these complexities are not enough, there are several other internal problems to consider. As noted by Yunker (1983), McInnes (1971), Stobaugh (1973) and others, one problem concerns the evaluation of management performance. How does an MNE evaluate properly the profit performance of a foreign subsidiary manager whose operations show a loss when in fact it was parent company executives who decided that the manager buy at artificially high transfer prices and sell at artificially low prices in order to shift profit to another subsidiary in a lower-tax country? And how does an MNE compare the performance of two managers who operate under exactly opposite conditions and instructions? One solution is to evaluate what a manager's performance would have been if the subsidiary had operated as an autonomous profit centre — that is, had all its internal transfers been at market prices or their equivalents. However, this method requires separate records for performance evaluation and considerable estimation, clerical effort and time.

The same sort of evaluation problems arise when parent executives want to know the *real* financial strength and position of individual companies within the corporate family. Obviously, the classic profit-centre analysis has its shortcomings when internal transfers are substantial and not at arm's-length (market) prices. An alternative to the profit-centre concept is the concept of 'contribution to the whole', in which subsidiaries and managers are evaluated in terms of their contribution to the MNE's overall global position. This calls for the evaluation of managers not in terms of subsidiaries' profitability but in terms of their effectiveness in achieving the specific objectives assigned to them. However, this method also requires considerable bookkeeping and diverse internal evaluation and reporting procedures.

As observed by Coburn, Ellis and Milano (1981), another major internal problem concerns the sheer cost and complexity of internal pricing decisions and their myriad results. For a large multinational firm, an enormous amount of time and effort is required to determine and evaluate its transfer pricing strategies in terms of prices, flows, methods and timings of payments. With dozens of subsidiaries handling hundreds of product lines in an assortment of constantly changing environments, there is an incentive to keep transfer pricing simple and systematic. An additional incentive is the number and seniority of the personnel who would have to be involved in developing and evaluting transfer price strategy and in the attendant bookkeeping. And as Coburn, Ellis and Milano (1981) noted, the sheer cost of designing, organising, and operating a complex transfer pricing system may make the undertaking not worth the effort. Some proof of this can be found in the transfer pricing systems actually in use. As Arpan (1972, Ch. 4) has reported, most of the world's multinational companies use relatively unsophisticated systems, and many do not consciously use them in any manner other than they would with unaffiliated buyers or sellers. And as is discussed in Section 8.4, the ability of multinational firms to utilise complex, manipulative transfer pricing systems is increasingly constrained by the governments of the countries in which they operate.

8.4 The Critical Impact of Governments

Governments are not all alike, nor are they all equally concerned about inter-corporate prices and their effects. As noted in Arpan's study, the Japanese, French and Italian governments appear to rank among the least concerned; the United States, Canada and a majority of developing countries rank among the most concerned. The government attitude is important to a multinational in terms of its business–government relations. In the current world atmosphere of nationalistic fever and fervour, the position of multinationals is increasingly perilous. As a consequence, they are increasingly on the defensive in terms of justifying their presence and demonstrating their benefits to the countries concerned. Most governments, rightly or wrongly, view market-based transfer prices as less manipulative, less suspicious, more fair and hence more desirable than cost-based transfer prices. As a result, companies using arm's-length prices have one area less of contention and possible conflict with governments.

As Burns and Ross (1981) have reported, in an increasing number of countries, including Canada, West Germany, the USA and the UK, national governments are requiring market-price equivalents for international inter-corporate transfers. In some countries, government officials have the authority to adjust non-market-based transfer prices to determine the proper tariff to be assessed. In others, they have the power to reallocate income in order to determine the income to be taxed.

Sections 402 and 402(A) of the Tariff Act and Section 482 of the United States Internal Revenue Service Code clearly specify arm's-length (market-price-based) prices for inter-corporate transfers, both domestic and international. Under Section 482, the burden of proof is on companies to justify their use of prices other than arm's-length prices, and the tax commissioner is empowered to reallocate income in order to arrive at a reasonable division of income even if market prices were ostensibly used. Section 69 of Canada's tax law, and Section 485 of the UK's tax law also pertain directly to international transfer prices, although neither country has gone as far as the United States in formalising guidelines to define an arm's-length price. In West Germany, Section 1 of the Foreign Tax Law is directed solely toward international transactions between related parties, and complements Section 8 of the Corporate Income Tax Law. Non-arm's-length prices are deemed to contain a hidden profit that is treated as a constructive dividend, but there are no legislated guidelines or regulations interpreting the arm's-length standard.

In short, governments are not standing idly by. Whereas once they confined themselves to verbal criticisms, now they act. Some examples provided by Carley (1974) are:

1. Members of the Tokyo High Prosecutor's Office confiscated some 1,500 sets of files from the headquarters of Shell's subsidiary to begin an investigation of its oil pricing policies there.
2. In West Germany, members of the Berlin Cartel Office have investigated paper and drug prices that multinationals were charging their German subsidiaries.
3. The British government, as part of the 1975 Finance Act, issued new tax regulations regarding transfer prices being set in connection with the sale of North Sea oil.
4. In the United States the Federal Energy Administration started administrative action against Gulf Oil Corporation. Gulf was alleged to have overcharged itself for oil purchased from certain of its foreign subsidiaries to keep profits out of the United States and thus reduce its US tax bill.
5. Developing countries are also getting into the act. IBM's transfer pricing practices are under investigation in a number of such nations.

On a multilateral level, the 24-nation Organisation for Economic Cooperation and Development (OECD) in 1979 issued a report on 'Transfer Pricing and Multinational Enterprises', which attempted to describe generally agreed practices in determining transfer prices for tax purposes. The report's basic premise is that all such transactions must conform to the arm's-length principle, and it draws heavily on the US regulations.

Increased government concern and action are making it not only difficult but also dangerous for firms to manipulate transfer prices. In addition, government officials have become more sophisticated about transfer pricing. So, while the incentives for manipulation still remain, the opportunities have decreased and the penalties have increased. This is not to say that there are no longer benefits to be derived from transfer price manipulation or that firms have ceased doing it. The heyday of transfer price manipulation is probably over, but transfer pricing will remain highly significant for multinationals and their financial and accounting staff.

National Differences in Transfer Pricing Systems

There is some evidence that the nationality of the parent company affects the transfer pricing system utilised by multinationals and the relative importance given to the various factors considered in establishing transfer prices. An early study by Arpan (1972) of the transfer pricing systems of 60 multinationals based in different countries drew these conclusions.

1. American, French, British and Japanese managements seemed to prefer cost-oriented transfer prices, while Canadians, Italians, and Scandinavians preferred market prices. No particular orientation or preference along either line was discernible for German, Belgian, Swiss or Dutch multinationals. Overall, however, the transfer pricing systems of non-US-based multinationals were less complex and more market-oriented than American systems.
2. Although non-US-based companies generally considered the same environmental variables when formulating guidelines for transfer prices, among the larger companies there were distinguishable national differences in the relative importance attached to each of these considerations. These differences are summarised in Table 8.2.

   As can be seen from the table, American, Canadian, French and Italian companies considered income taxes to be the most important variable affecting transfer pricing policy, while British companies considered the improvement of the financial appearance of their US subsidiaries as most important. With the exception of Scandinavian companies, inflation was also identified as an important variable in transfer pricing policies.
3. In contrast to the external influences just mentioned, non-US-based multinationals considered only about half as many internal parameters as their American counterparts did. With the exception of the British, most firms in the study viewed transfer pricing more as a means of controlling subsidiary operations than as a technique for motivating and evaluating subsidiary performance. This is largely explained by the fact that the use of the profit-centre concept was not widespread among non-US-based companies. Aside from control, one consideration deemed important by all firms was the acceptability of transfer prices to both host and parent country governments.

Table 8.2 Differences in Importance of Variables in Transfer Price Determination

	Parent Nationality						
	USA	*Canada*	*France*	*West Germany*	*Italy*	*Scandinavia*	*UK*
Income tax	1	1	1	3	1	3	3
Customs duties	2	2	2	3	3	3	3
Inflation	1	2	2	2	2	3	2
Changes in currency exchange rates	3	3	2	2	3	3	2
Exchange controls	2	3	5	5	5	5	5
Improving financial appearance of subsidiary	3	3	3	4	4	4	1
Expropriation	3	3	5	5	5	5	5
Export subsidies and tax credits	4	2	2	4	2	4	2
Level of competition	4	2	2	3	2	3	3

Source: Arpan (1972).
Notes: Weighting Scale:
1 = high importance
2 = medium importance
3 = low importance
4 = not mentioned
5 = mentioned only with respect to non-US operations

8.5 Accountants and Transfer Pricing

Accountants are involved in several areas pertaining to international transfer pricing. They are responsible for providing appropriate data for cost-based transfer prices, even though it is typically personnel at high corporate levels who finally determine the transfer prices to be used. In instances of governmental investigation or litigation, accountants are called upon to explain and justify the methods used to derive transfer prices. If other than arm's-length transfer prices are used, accountants typically are involved in preparing performance reports to management showing what the profitability of an operation would have been if arm's-length prices had been used. And, in countries that require consolidated financial reports for tax or financial reporting purposes, accountants must eliminate profits arising from inter-corporate transfers. Inter-corporate profits arise from the transfer of inventories, properties or other assets (1) between companies included in the consolidated statement, (2) between such companies and investee companies accounted for under the equity method of accounting, and (3) between investee companies accounted for under the equity method. Failure to eliminate inter-company profits distorts the financial results of operations, overstating the profit of one unit while understating the profit of another. As but one example of the difference in 'reported profits' that can result, Toshiba Corporation of Japan once showed an unconsolidated net income of $30 million which would have been a $13 million net loss on a consolidated basis with inter-company transactions netted out.

8.6 Conclusion

International transfer pricing has grown in importance with international business expansion. It remains a powerful tool with which multinational companies can achieve a wide variety of corporate objectives. At the same time, international transfer pricing can cause relations to deteriorate between multinationals and governments because some of the objectives achievable through transfer price manipulation are at odds with government objectives. Complex manipulated transfer pricing systems can also make the evaluation of subsidiary performance difficult and can take up substantial amounts of costly, high-level management time.

Yet despite these problems and an inherent desire to keep things simple, the advantages of transfer price manipulation remain considerable, given the market imperfections of today's international business environment. These advantages keep international transfer pricing high on the list of important decision areas for multinational firms. Accountants will therefore need to know about transfer pricing, be they employed by multinational firms, national tax authorities, other involved governmental agencies, or public accounting firms.

References

Arpan, J.S. (1972) *International Intracorporate Pricing: Non-American Systems and Views*, Praeger.

Burns, J. and Ross, R. (1981) 'Establishing international transfer pricing standards for tax audits of multinational enterprises', *International Journal of Accounting*, Volume 17 (1), Fall.

Carley, W.M. (1974) 'Profit probes: investigations beset multinational firms with stress on pricing', *Wall Street Journal*, 19 December.

Coburn, D.L., Ellis, J.K. and Milano, D.R. (1981) 'Dilemmas in MNC transfer pricing', *Management Accounting*, November.

Keegan, W.J. (1969) 'Multinational pricing: how far is arm's-length?', *Columbia Journal of World Business*, May–June.

Lessard, D.R. (1985) 'Transfer prices, taxes, and financial markets: implications of international financial transfers within the multinational corporation', in Donald R. Lessard (ed.) *International Financial Management: Theory and Application*, 2nd edn, John Wiley.

McInnes, J.M. (1971) 'Financial control systems for multinationals: an empirical investigation', *Journal of International Business Studies*, Fall.

Nobes, C.W. and Parker, R.H. (1985) *Comparative International Accounting*, 2nd edn, Philip Allan.

Rugman, A.M. and Eden, L. (eds), (1985) *Multinationals and Transfer Pricing*, St. Martin's Press.

Rutenberg, D. (1970) 'Manoeuvering liquid assets in multinational companies: formulation and deterministic solution procedures', *Management Science*, June.

Stobaugh, R. (1973) 'The bent measuring stick for foreign subsidiaries', *Harvard Business Review*, Vol. 51, September/October.

Thomas, A. (1971) 'Transfer prices of the multinational firm: when will they be arbitrary?', *Abacus*, June.

United Nations (1978) *Transnational Corporations in World Development: A Re-examination*, United Nations, New York.

US Tariff Commission (1973) *Implications of Multinational Firms for World Trade and Investment and for US Trade and Labor*, (Report to the Committee on Finance of the US Senate and its Subcommittee on International Trade), Government Printing Office, Washington.

Yunker, P.J. (1983) 'A survey study of subsidiary autonomy, performance evaluation and transfer pricing in multinational corporations', *Columbia Journal of World Business*, Fall.

Further Reading

Arpan, J.S. (1973) 'Multinational firm pricing in international markets', *Sloan Management Review*, Winter 1972–73.

Arpan, J.S. and Radebaugh, L. (1984) *International Accounting and Multinational Enterprises*, Ch. 8, John Wiley.

Barrett, M.E.O. (1977) 'The case of the tangled transfer price', *Harvard Business Review*, May–June.

Casey, M.P. (1985) 'International transfer pricing', *Management Accounting*, October.

Fantl, I.L. (1974) 'Transfer pricing — tread carefully', *CPA Journal*, Vol. 44, December.

Greene, J. (1969) 'Intercompany pricing across national frontiers', *Conference Board Record*, October.

Greene, J. and Duerr, M.G. (1970) *Intercompany Transactions in the Multinational Firm*, Conference Board, New York.

Milburn, J.A. (1976) 'International transfer transactions: what price?', *CA Magazine*, Canada, December.

Schulman, J.S. (1969) 'Transfer pricing in the multinational firm', *European Business*, January.

Watts, G.C., Hammer, R.M. and Burge, M. (1977) *Accounting for the Multinational Corporation*, Ch. 4, Financial Executives Research Foundation, New York.

Index